Helping Children
Cope with
Divorce

Helping Children Cope with Divorce

Edward Teyber

California State University
San Bernardino

Jossey-Bass Publishers • San Francisco

FIRST JOSSEY-BASS PAPERBACK EDITION PUBLISHED IN 1996
THIS BOOK WAS ORIGINALLY PUBLISHED BY LEXINGTON BOOKS

Substantial discounts on bulk quantities of Jossey-Bass books are
available to corporations, professional associations, and other
organizations. For details and discount information, contact the
special sales department at Jossey-Bass Inc., Publishers
(415) 433-1740; Fax (800) 605-2665.

For sales outside the United States, please contact your local
Simon & Schuster International Office.

Jossey-Bass Web address: http://www.josseybass.com

Manufactured in the United States of America on Lyons Falls
Pathfinder Tradebook. This paper is acid-free and 100 percent
totally chlorine-free.

Library of Congress Cataloging-in-Publication Data

Teyber, Edward.
Helping children cope with divorce / Edward Teyber.
p.   cm.
ISBN 0-669-27068-7
1. Children of divorced parents—United States.   2. Divorced
parents—United States.   I. Title.
HQ777.5.T49   1992
306.89—dc20   92-18286
                                                      CIP

FIRST EDITION

Paperback Printing 10 9 8

Hardcover Printing 10 9 8 7 6 5 4 3 2

For Ted and Reed

Contents

9. Parentification: Turning Children into Adults   163

10. Child-Rearing Practices   179

11. Step-Families: Forming New Family Relationships   202

PART ONE

Introduction

You Can Help Your Children Successfully Adjust to Divorce

This book teaches divorcing parents what they can do to help their children successfully adjust to divorce. The biggest concern for almost all divorcing parents is whether their children will be hurt by the breakup. To be sure, divorce brings painful feelings that will be difficult for every family member to deal with. Children do not understand the changes that are occurring, and they are afraid of what is going to happen to them. Although parents are usually unaware of this, children are also worried about the well-being of their parents, who now seem so angry and sad. Regardless of who initiated the divorce, most parents are also profoundly upset by the separation. In addition to their own personal distress, they are burdened by guilt over breaking up the family and by feelings of inadequacy because they do not know how to reassure their children. However, these and other problems are resolvable, and parents can take control of this challenging family crisis and do a great deal to help their children.

I am going to be your child's advocate in the pages ahead. I will communicate to you—the concerned parent—what your children may be thinking, feeling, and needing throughout the different stages of divorce. At the same time that I help you understand the questions and concerns that divorce arouses for children, I will also provide practical guidelines to help you respond more effectively. If you follow the guidelines suggested here, it will go a very long way toward helping your children successfully adjust to divorce.

In this introduction, I first examine the broad historical and social changes that have transformed the American family and led to a soaring divorce rate. The next section summarizes the effects of divorce on children and reviews how children at different ages tend to react to their parent's breakup. The final section of this introduction addresses the far-reaching impact of divorce on parents. In particular, I examine parents' guilt and pain over the divorce and identify the different stages of adjustment that parents often go through. In contrast to this more general introductory chapter, each of the chapters that follow focus on a specific divorce-related problem and provide concrete steps to resolve it.

The Changing American Family

As the divorce rate has soared in the past twenty-five years, most of us have either personally experienced or shared with a friend the disruption of marriage and family. Divorce has become so widespread in the 1990s that over one-third of children today will experience a parental divorce. How will divorce affect these children? Are there typical reactions and predictable problems that boys and girls will have because of their parents' divorce? What can parents do to help their children cope with divorce and adjust to family relationships after the divorce? The pages that follow answer these questions and many more.

Divorcing parents need specific information and practical guidelines to help with the questions and problems that divorce brings up for children. My goal in this book is to help parents anticipate the concerns that divorce typically arouses for children, understand what these problems mean for their children, and teach parents how they can respond effectively to them. For example, I teach parents how to explain the divorce to their children, suggest custody and living arrangements that will be in the children's best interest, and provide guidelines to help shield children from parental conflicts. This straightforward approach will make divorce easier for both children and parents alike.

Before we embark on this important journey, however, we need to learn some other things about divorce. In particular, parents need to understand why so many divorces are occurring today. Are people too selfish to care about others anymore? Have people today become too lazy to work on the problems that exist in every relationship? Although divorcing parents are sometimes blamed in these ways, social demographers and family historians tell us that the explanations for the soaring divorce rate are not so simple.

A Historical Perspective on the Family

Let's take the long view for a moment and see what family historians have to tell us about the current crisis in the American family. In recent years, researchers have uncovered a great deal of historical evidence of what family life was like in previous centuries. These statistical records and archival materials from the eighteenth and nineteenth centuries show that family conflict and instability are not modern characteristics. As far back as the records go, there is unmistakable evidence that family life was fraught with conflict and tensions, subject to dramatic fluctuations, and full of diversity. It is a romantic misperception to idealize the family of the past as a safe haven.

But such discoveries do not mean that profound changes in family life and the fabric of society have not occurred. Urbanization and industrialization in the twentieth century, women entering the work force during and after World War II, and control over fertility through birth control in the 1960s have all contributed to a shift in traditional roles, responsibilities, and decision-making power in the family. As a result, the divorce rate doubled between 1960 and 1975, and in the 1990s there are now over 1.1 million divorces annually. Although the divorce rate peaked in 1979, it has leveled off at a very high rate. One out of two new marriages in the United States will eventually end in divorce, most of them within the first ten years (In certain counties in California the ratio is as high as two out of three.) Because this high rate of divorce is expected to continue, over one-third of children today will experience a parental divorce.

Divorce is often misconstrued as a circumscribed or terminal event that ends when the judge drops the gavel. However, divorcing parents will find that the divorce is but one phase in a series of family transitions. Although the divorce rate is high, people have not given up on marriage. About eighty percent of men and seventy-five percent of women will eventually remarry, usually within three years after the divorce (sixty percent of these remarriages will also end in divorce at some point, however). As a result of the high remarriage rate, twenty-five percent of children today will eventually spend some time living in a step-family. Divorcing parents face different challenges with their children at each of these different stages. In the chapters that follow, I help parents respond to the changing concerns that children have when their parents initially break up, while living in a single-parent household or going back and forth between two homes, and when they are becoming part of a new step-family.

The Child's Experience of Divorce

The three brief scenarios that follow show the typical responses of each family member to marital disruption. In each situation you will see certain problems beginning to emerge for the children involved. Ask yourself, as you read along, how you would respond if these were your children.

THE ABBOTT FAMILY. Although Jack felt bad about leaving his wife, Linda, and hurting their two children, he had made up his mind to go. He planned to move into an apartment with his girlfriend by the weekend. "I know this is hard for you," Jack began, and then he abruptly announced that he wanted a divorce.

Linda felt as if she had been kicked in the stomach. "What are you saying? Why are you leaving us? Why didn't you tell me?" Stunned and confused, she was almost unable to take in what he was saying.

Two months later it still seemed to Linda as if her life had fallen apart. Although Jack had originally suggested that they remain "friends," Linda was bitter and unresponsive. She repeatedly told her daughters that their father had betrayed them and they shouldn't have anything to do with him. And, as if humiliating her had not been enough, Jack was going to try to take her daughters away from her, too. Linda simply couldn't believe it: He was going to seek joint custody of the two girls.

Shortly after the separation, Linda and Jack's daughters' behavior began to change. Thirteen-year-old Marta was angry at everyone and everything. She had sided with her mother and wouldn't see or speak to her father, despite his repeated requests to visit her. Marta blamed her father and hated him for leaving. Yet, even though Marta took her mother's side against her father, she gradually began to distance herself from her mother as well. Marta began to spend little time at home, her school grades plummeted, and Linda started receiving reports that her daughter was not attending her classes regularly.

Unlike Marta, her eight-year-old sister, Ann, wasn't angry all the time. Instead, she was very sad. Ann felt torn apart inside and was praying that her parents would get back together again. She reasoned that if Marta weren't so angry at Dad, it would be easier for him to move back home.

Ann also felt torn between her parents. She missed seeing her father, and they often talked secretly on the phone. Ann felt guilty, however, and thought, "If Mom knew, she'd think I was on Dad's side. But I want to see Dad. He tells me it's unfair of Mom to make him into the bad guy. But Mom's right, he left us and he wouldn't have if he really loved us. I don't know who's right or who's wrong. I don't know what to do. I feel pulled in two directions." Ann directed her conflict inward and began to suffer from stomachaches.

THE BAXTER FAMILY. When Joan's marriage broke up, her husband moved out of the state without leaving a forwarding address. Joan was left to raise and support their four-year-old son, Ben. In the four months since he had left, her husband Jim had sent only two support checks. Joan felt abandoned and frantic because she didn't know how she was going to make ends meet. Her county welfare check wasn't enough to pay for food, rent, and the car payment each month, so Joan had gotten a job as a salesclerk to make ends meet. However, by the time she had paid for daycare for Ben there wasn't enough money left over.

Joan felt overwhelmed by her life. Even her son was completely out of control. "Ben is driving me crazy," Joan told a relative. "Ever since his father left, I can't control him—he won't do anything I say. It's awful. He fights with me constantly, yet he won't leave me alone for a minute. He throws a temper tantrum when I drop him off at the daycare center, even though he used to like going there. He used to go to bed easily at night. Now putting him to bed is a struggle that takes most of the evening. He wants just one more drink of water, one more story, one more light turned on. I just don't have anything left to give and Ben wants more, more, more.

"I've finally given up trying to keep him in his own bed. He wakes up from a nightmare and won't stop crying until I let him climb into bed with me. Then in the morning he still won't obey me. I tell you I can't control this boy anymore since his father left. He's ruining my life!"

When his father first left, Ben felt sad and missed him. Then, after the first week or so, Ben just felt angry. He kept thinking to himself, "Why did Dad leave me? I hate him for going away. I don't ever want him to come back." Sometimes Ben felt angry at his mother too: Maybe it was her fault that his father had left. Ben's feelings were confusing and scary. Being angry at his mother was the scariest thing in the whole world and made Ben afraid that he might drive away his mother as he had his father. He thought, "If Dad left because he didn't want me, maybe Mom will leave, too! Then I'll be all alone and there won't be anybody to feed me or take care of me." Ben knew it was very important not to let his mother get very far away from him.

THE CAMPBELL FAMILY. One month after her thirtieth birthday, Barbara asked Dave for a divorce. Dave wanted to stay together, but Barbara insisted that she needed "more out of life" than she had. Barbara wanted to go back to school and develop a career that would make her more independent than she had been with Dave. They had married immediately after high school, and she felt she had never had the chance to become her own person. Although Barbara didn't know exactly what she wanted, she felt strongly that what she had shared with Dave wasn't enough for her.

Six months later, Dave still didn't know what to do with his four- and eight-year-old sons, Danny and Mark, when they visited him at his new apartment. He usually took them to the movies or a ballgame, but nobody seemed to have much fun. And Dave would feel very frustrated when Danny started crying because he wanted to go home to his mother. He had always felt helpless when his boys were sad or cried. Barbara had always taken care of those needs, just as she had always fed and bathed and done almost everything else for them. Taking care of small children was natural for her. She always seemed to know exactly what to do, whereas Dave always felt as if he couldn't ever quite give what his children needed.

On top of feeling like a failure as a father, Dave was growing increasingly resentful toward both his former wife and his children. Dave told a friend, "I spend more than I can afford taking them out to eat and to movies and ballgames, and then they don't even talk to me. And when I take the boys back to their mother, she tells me she resents having to be the disciplinarian while I'm the Disneyland Daddy who just has fun with the kids. Barbara actually told Danny and Mark that the only reason she doesn't take them out the way I do is that I don't give her enough money!"

Dave started to see his sons less frequently.

Eight-year-old Mark had been very sad since his father moved out. Even though he got to see his father on weekends, their time together just wasn't the same as it used to be. Mark thought that everything would be all right if his parents would just get married again. Mark felt terrible because his mom often cried. Somehow, he felt, he had to find a way to keep her from crying. That's when he remembered that whenever he got into trouble, his parents had stopped fighting with each other and paid attention to him. Then they had gotten along better for a while.

Later that week Barbara got the first note from Mark's teacher that he had been fighting at school.

Even though divorce has become commonplace, it remains a terribly painful experience, as shown in the typical reactions to divorce just profiled. The prevailing theme of these three scenarios is the struggle each mother, father, and child faces with painful feelings of guilt and anger, failure and fear, sadness and loss. However, divorcing parents should be reassured that many of the concerns that Marta, Ann, Ben, Danny, and Mark expressed could be reduced or eliminated if their parents had known what to do. Parents who learn how to respond to their children before, during, and after the divorce can greatly reduce the insecurity, conflict, and pain that children experience.

The Effects of Divorce on Children

As we have seen, divorce has become prevalent, but what are its effects on children? Many talented researchers began studying this question in the 1970s, and their findings have provided a great deal of information about children and divorce. One thing researchers have learned is that we must distinguish between children's immediate, or short-term, reactions to marital separation and their long-term (more than two years) reactions. (Children's long-term reactions vary greatly, depending primarily on how the parents respond to the child during and after the separation. In particular, the amount of parental harmony or disharmony children experience after divorce will be the most important determinant of their long-term adjustment. In contrast, children's short-term reactions tend to be more uniform.

Short-Term Reactions

Researchers have found that almost all children are very upset by the initial breakup. When looking back on their childhoods, most adults whose parents divorced later describe the initial period of separation when one parent moved out as the most stressful time in their lives. Children usually do not understand what is happening, even though they may know many other children who have gone through divorce. Routinely, children are initially shocked and surprised by the separation, even though it seems clear to the adults that it did not happen suddenly. Boys tend to find the initial separation period more upsetting than girls. Despite the fact that there may have been a great deal of fighting, tension, or unhappiness in the home, children do not want the divorce. They do not find relief in it or welcome it in any way unless they have been witnessing physical violence.

During the first year after marital disruption, parents will see more anger, fear, depression, and guilt in their children. These troubled reactions will usually lessen by the second year. However, to understand children's short-term reactions to divorce more clearly, we must examine how the impact of divorce varies between boys and girls and how it affects children differently at different ages.

PRESCHOOLERS. Preschool children (aged three to five) often react to their parents' separation with both anger and sadness. Boys tend to become noisier, angrier, and more restless. They may not play as well with friends and tend to sit alone more often. Boys often disrupt group activities at nursery school rather than cooperating in group activities with other children. Some preschool girls will be angry, too, but others will become little adults. These "perfect" little girls become overly concerned with being neat and good and may lecture or scold other children as if they were a parent or teacher. Both boys and girls at this young age will feel sad, cry more often, and become more demanding.

In response to the initial shock of marital disruption, children will also regress—act younger than their age. That is, they will return to behavior that they had previously outgrown. For example, children may resume sucking their thumbs, carrying a security blanket, asking for a pacifier, hitting their siblings, or needing help to feed themselves. Further, these children will also feel more anxious or insecure. When three- to five-year-old children are anxious, for example, parents will observe more nightmares, bedwetting, masturbating, and fear about leaving the parent. As we discuss in more detail in chapter 2, these children have a very understandable fear. Having seen one parent move out unexpectedly, they are frightened of being left by the other parent as well.

SCHOOL-AGED. Divorce seems to be especially difficult for six-to eight-year-old children. Boys at this age are especially upset by the breakup and will usually be more distressed than girls. The primary reaction of these children is sadness. They are most likely to cry openly about the marital disruption and will often be sad and weepy. They tend to long for the out-of-home parent, and boys may miss their fathers particularly intensely. At this age, children are especially prone to believe that they have been rejected by the departing parent. This intense feeling of rejection and being unlovable results in lowered self-esteem, depression, and all—too often—a sharp decline in school performance. These children are worried about their parents, have trouble concentrating in school, and often try to prevent the divorce and restore their family.

Whereas the primary feeling for six-to eight-year-olds is sadness, it changes to anger for nine- to twelve-year-olds. These children may be intensely angry at both parents for the breakup or especially angry at the parent who initiated the separation. These children are prone to taking sides with one parent against the other and to assigning blame. As detailed in chapter 8, these children are especially vulnerable to becoming embroiled in destructive parental battles in which one parent seeks to blame, harass, or get revenge on the other. Unfortunately, many parents actively enlist children in these destructive parental battles.

As well as aligning with one parent against the other, these children also express anger in other ways. Many single-parent mothers report that it is impossible to discipline their nine- to twelve-year-old sons. In addition, these children may angrily reject their out-of-home father's attempts to spend time with them.

Anger is not the only reaction of these children, however. They are also sad about the breakup, afraid about what is going to happen, and lonely. In particular, children at this age feel powerless. They do not want the divorce, miss their intact families, long for the out-of-home parent, and feel helpless to alter the enormous changes occurring in their lives. Fueled by angry defiance and profound feelings of helplessness, school performance drops markedly for about one half of the children in this age group. Other symptoms may emerge during this age period as well. For example, many children will begin to have trouble getting along with their friends or will begin expressing physical complaints such as headaches and stomachaches. And, as discussed in chapter 10, some of these children also become so concerned about taking care of a parent and meeting their parent's need that they sacrifice their own welfare. For many reasons that we will examine later, marital disruption is a greater problem for sons than daughters in this age group.

Finally, strong gender differences have been found in school-aged children's reactions to divorce. In the two years following divorce, boys from divorced homes are far more likely to be in conflict with their mothers and disobey them than boys from intact homes. In contrast, school-aged girls from divorced families are more likely to function well and get along well with their custodial mothers. This tendency for boys to be more aggressive and uncooperative both at home and at school seems to occur in part because ninety percent of children live with their mothers after divorce. This means that girls retain their same-sex identification figure, whereas boys often lose theirs. This loss is further exacerbated because most fathers do not assume an active parenting role after divorce. For these and other reasons, most researchers have found that divorce is more problematic for boys than girls. However, as examined in chapter 6, problems for daughters do occur, but they are more apt to emerge (1) in adolescence as they begin dating and exploring heterosexual relationships and (2) when they enter a step-family.

ADOLESCENCE. Adolescence is a special time of life, and adolescents can respond very differently to their parents' divorce. On the one hand, adolescents often adjust to the family disruption better than younger children. Because they are becoming more independent and removed from family relations, they do not need as much affection and guidance as younger children. Adolescents usually cope with the divorce by distancing themselves from the parental relationship and becoming more involved in their own plans and future. Refreshingly, some adolescents show a positive developmental spurt in response to the marital disruption. These young people are often very helpful to their parents and younger siblings during this family crisis. Their own maturity and compassion can be seen as they participate constructively in family decisions, help with household responsibilities, and provide stable, nurturing relationships to younger siblings.

On the other hand, however, many adolescents initially feel betrayed by the divorce. Some adolescents will angrily disengage from the family and may begin acting out sexually, especially when they see that their parents have readily become involved in sexual relationships. Other adolescents may become depressed, withdraw from peers and family involvement, or lose their plans and ambitions for their own futures. Like older school-aged children, adolescents are also likely to have problems when they are pulled into loyalty conflicts and feel they must take sides or choose one parent over the other.

For most adolescents, however, the main concern is about their own future. In particular, they often worry about how the marital failure will influence their own future ability to have a good marriage or their ability to go to college. Because divorce is far more likely to occur when children are younger, most of our attention will be given to pre-adolescent children.

Longer-Term Reactions

A few research studies have looked at the long-term effects of divorce on children five to ten years after the divorce, and when children of divorce are in their late 20s and early 30s. At every time period, a similar pattern emerges: about thirty percent are doing very well, about forty percent have mixed successes and problems, and about thirty percent are struggling with significant, enduring problems. Many different themes are found in these long-term reactions to divorce, however. Some individuals remain angry with or rejecting of the departing parent; some feel sad and long for a parent who was uninvolved after the divorce; others hold onto unrealistic, idealized memories of the intact family. Some see themselves as needy and having been deprived of a childhood. Others, however, see themselves as stronger and more independent as a result of the divorce. Understandably, many adult children of divorce have heightened concerns about issues of trust, loyalty, and security in relationships. They also report more loneliness as adults and more marital conflict than the children of intact families.

The long-term effects of divorce are also more problematic for young adult men than women. As adults, these sons of divorce report more anxiety, worry, insomnia, and physical complaints, such as headaches and stomachaches; in addition, they tend to be less involved with their own children.

What does all of this mean to you, the concerned divorced parent? Do your children have to suffer the life-long consequences of your marital failure? No, absolutely not! Divorce does not have to harm children or cause long-term problems. The same parenting skills that lead to good adjustment in intact families will lead to good adjustment in divorced families. The quality of parenting you provide and your response to your child throughout the divorce are the most important determinants of your child's adjustment. Your children are likely to develop behavioral problems and long-term emotional conflicts if, for example, they are exposed to continuing parental fighting, lose emotional or physical contact with a parent after the divorce, are forced to take sides and choose between their parents, have little effective discipline, or are subtly coerced to meet their parent's emotional needs. In contrast, if children receive affection and consistent discipline, maintain good relationships with both parents, are not embroiled in parental conflicts, and so forth, they will adjust well. If parents can follow the parenting guidelines offered in the chapters that follow, children can make a secure and successful adjustment. It is not the divorce itself that causes problems for children, but the way parents respond to the children during the divorce and the quality of parenting they provide afterward.

Divorce is Painful for Parents

Although I act as your children's advocate in the pages ahead and focus on what you can do to help your children adjust, I don't ignore or forget the parents' difficulties. It is often easier to see and empathize with a child's pain than an adult's. However, parents have as much need and right to be understood and responded to as children. Before looking any further at the typical reactions of children to divorce and how parents can respond to them, I want to acknowledge how difficult divorce is for parents. It usually takes far longer for parents to adjust to the divorce than they had anticipated, and parents often go through a predictable series of stages in the divorce process. One of the biggest burdens that divorce brings to many parents is guilt.

The Divorce Process Takes Several Years

Researchers have observed wide mood swings, from elation to severe depression, in parents responding to the initial breakup. Parents typically report that poor work performance, health problems, anxiety, and sleep disturbances accompany the breakup. Parents also feel insecure in dating at this time and there is an increased rate of sexual dysfunction in men. Unfortunately, parents report increased smoking, drinking, and drug use during this stressful time.

Parents should be aware that the intense turmoil and disruption brought on by the initial breakup will settle down, but that they will not adjust to the divorce in a matter of weeks or even months.

Researchers have found that one year after the separation is often a low point for parents, and that it often takes as long as two or three years for divorcing parents to regain confidence and self-esteem.

Thus, parents should not place unrealistic expectations on themselves. Most parents will be distressed and upset for a much longer period than they think they should be. Statements like, "I've been separated for ten months now, so why do I still feel like crying at the drop of a hat" are typical of this attitude. It takes two to three years for many parents to work through the emotional process of divorce. Many complex issues must be resolved, and some researchers have observed three distinct phases in this divorce process.

The initial stage of breaking up is perhaps the most painful period, especially for mothers. This phase includes the wrenching period of increasing conflict, tension, and dissatisfaction in the marriage that culminates in one party "wanting out" and deciding to divorce (usually the mother) and one party moving out (usually the father). Contrary to the widely held misconception, mothers initiate about seventy percent of all divorces that involve children. These mothers have often agonized over this decision for some time. In contrast, fathers may not experience the full emotional impact of the divorce until later in the process, when mothers may be on their way toward recovering.

This disruptive period is often chaotic and may cause parents to behave irrationally. Unfortunately, hurtful interactions occur in this initial stage that can linger for years and continue to influence the quality of parenting that divorced parents can maintain. This time is also often frightening for children. Perhaps one-half of all children see their parents yelling at each other, making ugly threats toward each other, and throwing and breaking things. Tragically, far too many children see their parents hitting each other in their hurt, betrayal, and rage. Common sense and good judgment tend to be abandoned during this stressful initial stage. For example, children may be inappropriately exposed to their parents' short-term sexual liaisons, or parents may act impulsively (for example, stealing children) in ways that create enduring, unresolvable hatred and bitter distrust.

This initial stage of marital disruption may last a few months or, in a few cases, it may drag on for a year or two. However, it is *very damaging* for children to witness intense and dramatic parental conflict. Separating parents can do much for their children by shielding them from such scenes. It is especially important during this initial period for parents to exercise restraint and plan arrangements for the breakup as thoughtfully as possible. There will be much less chaos when there is some mutual concern, respect, or trust between separating parents. Or, if one parent insists on "acting out," children will still fare far better if the other parent does not use this irresponsible behavior as license to respond in kind.

Specific guidelines are given later (especially in chapters 2 through 4) to help parents make careful plans for their children during this initial stage. If conflicts have already happened, however, there are still actions that parents can take to help redress their earlier mistakes.

As the chaos from the initial breakup settles down, many parents enter a new transitional stage. In this period of trial and error, parents try out new lifestyles and reorganize their lives. Many changes can occur for parents and children in this transitional period, which may last from a few months to a year or two. Parents may go back to school, re-enter the work force, change careers, buy and sell homes, and begin and end new relationships. Children may move to different neighborhoods, leave friends behind and make new ones, change schools, and go back and forth between two households with differing rules. Clearly, this is an uprooting, unsettling period because parents are often forced to move several times and children must cope with profound changes.

However, children will adjust better if they have more stability in their lives and fewer demands to deal with. Parents can help children cope by providing as much continuity, familiarity, and predictability in their lives as possible. That is, children will adjust better when parents can keep as many things as possible constant in their lives—for example, school, church, bedroom, babysitter, or playmates. Furthermore, children will adjust better when their daily lives are regulated by more structure and routine, consistent discipline, and dependable, regularly scheduled contact with both parents. When changes must occur, parents can help children adjust by giving repeated explanations and clear expectations for what is going to occur and when.

The third stage of parental divorce is a renewed sense of stability.

This phase happens sooner for some families than others, of course, and children will feel more secure as their parents can provide more stability. New love relationships for mother and father settle down, and stable patterns of visitation and support are established. As the dust settles, some children will be living in single-parent homes; some children will be going comfortably back and forth between two-parent homes; others will be living in step-families.

Clearly, divorce is painful for parents, and it is often going to take 2 or 3 years to come to terms with the far-reaching changes it brings. Many parents are going to find that the divorce is more upsetting, takes longer to adjust to, and changes much more in their lives than they had anticipated. This is usually true for both parents, regardless of who initiated the divorce. As divorcing parents struggle through the three phases of the divorce process, they also need support throughout these difficult transitions. One important step in the parents' adjustment is to come to terms with exaggerated feelings of guilt and blame.

Parental Guilt

STAYING TOGETHER FOR THE SAKE OF THE CHILDREN. One of the biggest problems for divorcing parents is their own sense of failure because they feel they have "let their children down." Almost every parent struggles with guilt about the divorce, even when the other spouse has initiated the breakup. Unfortunately, most parents accept our society's critical, blame-ridden attitudes toward divorcing parents. The divorcing parent's anguish is often expressed in words such as these: "My children have to suffer the consequences of my personal failure. It's selfish of me to seek a divorce that will cause pain and conflict for my children just to improve my own life. Wouldn't it be better to stay married for the sake of the children?"

Although people often have been brought up to believe that parents should stay together for the sake of the children, research does not support this belief. It is not in the children's best interests for unhappily married couples to stay together when this exposes their children to chronic marital conflict. Researchers have shown that children adjust better in split homes that function well than in conflict-ridden marriages. More specifically, a harmonious intact family is best for children, but a harmonious divorced environment is better than a disharmonious intact family. However, the evidence is also definitive that a disharmonious divorce after which the parents continue to battle is the worst environment of all for children. Both divorced and married parents need to be aware of the profoundly detrimental consequences for children of growing up with chronically embattled parents.

Decades of research on family interaction have repeatedly found that children are affected adversely by conflict and turmoil in their parents' marriage. Children are more likely to develop personality and behavioral problems in unhappy, unloving families in which the parents fight continually than in any other kind of family situation.

This chronic marital conflict is difficult for all children, but it seems to be especially hard for boys, who tend to develop behavioral problems as result. Boys who grow up in an atmosphere of continuing marital strife often become angry, defiant, and hard to discipline. They frequently get into trouble with the police and with school authorities. As young adults, these boys have been found to have an alarmingly high arrest rate for criminal behavior. Girls are also affected by marital conflict, and they also may become more aggressive and disobedient. In many cases, however, they will react by becoming anxious, withdrawn, or perfectionistically well-behaved.

In 1985, a nationwide survey of 1,423 children conducted by the National Institutes of Mental Health found that children who live with a divorced parent have fewer behavioral problems than those who live with married parents who always fight. Clearly, children living in families where there is constant conflict would be better off if their parents amicably went their separate ways. This finding goes a long way toward explaining why the most poorly adjusted children of divorce have bitter, litigious parents who continue fighting with each other in court or through the children.

But what about parents who are unhappily married but have the restraint and good sense to shield their children from fights, screaming, demeaning insults, ugly threats, or violence? Do children fare better in quietly unhappy, emotionally disengaged, but intact families than in divorced homes? The research literature is more ambiguous on this question, so we have to fall back more on personal values and preferences for an answer. Divorce will be painful for all children, and engender long-term problems for many. This cold, hard fact must be faced squarely. Because of the consequences for their children, parents should never make the decision to divorce impulsively or in anger. Much soul-searching, consultation with respected others, repeated attempts to directly address the problems in the marriage, and careful planning for the children must all come first. In weighing the decision to divorce or stay married, however, parents must consider several potentially harmful consequences of deciding to remain unhappily together.

First, children often shoulder a large burden of guilt and responsibility if they feel that their parents have stayed together unhappily for their sake. Second, staying in an unhappy marriage also teaches children to avoid problems by providing a role model of passivity, disappointment, and resignation to having less in life than they want. Finally, parents also have a right to their own happiness, and their needs must be considered as well. Thus, parents should not have to stay together for the sake of their children after honest efforts have repeatedly failed to resolve marital conflicts. That is not the end of the story, however. With rights come responsibilities, and parents must make a commitment to work together constructively in the child's best interest. As emphasized throughout this book, the marital relationship can end, but a responsible parenting relationship must continue.

PARENTAL GUILT UNDERMINES EFFECTIVE PARENTING. When parents do divorce because they are unhappily married, they often struggle with intense guilt. These feelings often are just as strong when the other spouse initiated the breakup. Too often, responsible parents who are devoted to doing the right thing for their children are ruled by unnecessary guilt. This exaggerated guilt and self-blame not only results in considerable anguish for parents, it also causes some very significant problems for children. Parental guilt over the divorce contributes to some of children's most common adjustment problems.

When parents feel too guilty about the breakup they cannot talk with their children about the divorce, although their children need them to do so. Chapters 2 through 4 demonstrate that children adjust better when they receive effective parental explanations that answer their basic questions about why the divorce is occurring and what is going to happen to them. Unfortunately, most parents cannot talk with their children about their concerns because it makes parents feel too guilty. Guilt-ridden parents simply want to avoid the topic and so they avoid their children's questions, insecurities, or sadness in order to manage their own guilt. As a consequence, children do not receive the support they need and will have more difficulty coping with the breakup.

Parental guilt also leads to other problems for children. For example, parents who are guilty about the divorce will be overly critical of themselves and may, at times, feel self-hatred, which leads to depression and causes parents to withdraw emotionally from their children and others. This response is especially problematic because guilty, self-punitive parents become depressed and less available to children at precisely the time when children feel insecure and in greater need of emotional contact with their parents.

Another way that parental guilt increases problems for children is by intensifying the conflict between the parents. It cannot be emphasized enough that children will be hurt when they are exposed to parental fighting or are forced to take sides or choose between their parents. Divorcing parents must take steps to insulate their children from whatever anger, distrust, and bitterness exist in the parental relationship. Guilt plays into this all-important issue of embroiling children in parental conflicts. We have just seen how some parents use guilt over the divorce to punish and blame themselves excessively. In contrast, some other parents try to deflect their guilt by blaming their former spouses for everything that went wrong in the marriage. These parents rigidly divert all the blame and cannot consider any valid criticisms because accepting any responsibility would open the floodgates of their own feelings of guilt, failure, and inadequacy. When this stance is taken, no parental conflicts can be talked about and resolved, and children are frightened by exposure to unrelenting parental battles.

Finally, parental guilt also undermines the parent's ability to discipline the child. Chapter 10 examines the effective child-rearing practices that parents should employ to help children successfully adjust to divorce. When parents are guilty about the divorce, however, they may find it hard to take a firm stand, say no, and effectively enforce the limits they have set. Children have more adjustment problems when parents are too guilty or insecure to tolerate the child's protest when they set limits and enforce rules. The following anecdote may help to demonstrate how guilt over the divorce can result in ineffective parenting and ruin a parent's personal life.

Although Mrs. Smith had been divorced for two years, she still felt guilty about letting her children down. Family finances were much tighter than they had been before the divorce, and Mrs. Smith felt especially guilty because she couldn't buy her teenage daughter, Sarah, many of the things her friends were getting from their parents.

Mrs. Smith had started working overtime just to avoid having to say no to her daughter so repeatedly. The extra money she earned helped her satisfy Sarah, but Mrs. Smith felt as if she didn't have enough time or energy left for all the other everyday tasks. And there certainly wasn't any time left for simply enjoying herself. Life had become a grim routine of meeting everyone else's needs, and Mrs. Smith became increasingly depressed by the burden of so many demands. Finally, she followed the advice of a coworker and met with a counselor.

Mrs. Smith's counselor was quick to point out all the ways in which her guilt over the divorce had diminished her life. In particular, the counselor noticed that Mrs. Smith's guilt was hampering her ability to effectively parent her son as well as her daughter. Nine-year-old David had acquired a behavior problem since the divorce (and, thus, had only confirmed Mrs. Smith's guilt). He disobeyed his mother and had recently been sent home from school for talking back to his teacher. The therapist helped Mrs. Smith realize that David's troubled behavior stemmed from her inability to enforce the rules and limits she had set for him rather than being just because of the divorce.

Mrs. Smith's guilt was interfering with her ability to take a firm stand and say no when necessary. Since she felt that she had hurt David by getting a divorce, she thought she needed to be more understanding and, therefore, more lenient with him. In addition, Mrs. Smith couldn't face David's resentment and rejection when she told him to do something he didn't want to do. This pattern of behavior had evolved to the point where David knew he could say and do almost anything he wanted to his mother and get away with it. The counselor pointed out that once children learn that they can defy a parent, they may not feel a need to obey teachers or other authority figures either.

In the next few sessions with the counselor, Mrs. Smith re-examined and finally put to rest her guilt about the divorce. Once this burden was behind her, she was better able to stand up to her son's criticism and complaints. With the counselor's guidance, she instituted a "time-out" program of discipline for her son and began to manage him effectively. When Mrs. Smith could no longer be manipulated by David, his behavior at school took a sharp turn for the better. For Mrs. Smith and many other parents, resolving this guilt over letting the children down allows them to parent more effectively and to have more realistic expectations of themselves.

How can we put realistic limits on irrational guilt and prevent the parenting problems that stem from it? One of the most important things divorcing parents must do is learn to separate the *event* (for example, the divorce, the remarriage, the relocation to a new city, the birth of a new sibling) from the *context,* or way, in which parents respond to the event and help children understand and cope with it. Let's examine this far-reaching distinction more carefully.

It does not tell us anything to say that a child is from an intact or divorced family. Children can adjust well or poorly in both types of families. Intact or divorced are not the essential issues. There can be parental cooperation, nurturance, consistent discipline, effective communication, and predictability in either type of family. These characteristics of family interaction, regardless of whether the family is intact or divorced, determine children's successful adjustment. Similarly, threats, loneliness, shaming, or competing alliances can exist in intact or divorced homes. These family interaction variables produce unhappy, nonachieving children with emotional and behavioral problems. Although this distinction between the event (the divorce) and the context (the way that parents respond to it) may seem only academic at first, subsequent chapters will show that it largely determines your child's adjustment to divorce. Furthermore, the ability to make this distinction gives parents their rightful opportunity to take charge of the divorce process rather than just being passively controlled by it.

Research findings show that about one-third of children have substantial problems in the years following divorce, another third have some moderate adjustment difficulties, and the final third adjust very well. In this context, it is important to realize that *children do not have to suffer long-term negative consequences of divorce.* Parents can effectively influence children's adjustment by following certain guidelines. This book gives parents the information they need to help their children and respond to the questions, concerns, and problems children typically have. Although the guidelines offered here are not a cure-all, parents can learn to do much for their children. If parents follow the guidelines suggested in the following pages, they will often see marked improvement in children who have been struggling with the impact of their parent's divorce. This educational program for divorcing parents is a practical, understandable, and basic plan of action. Most parents will find that they can successfully adopt these guidelines for dealing with their children.

Let's turn now to the first concern that troubles most young children of divorce—the fear of being left or abandoned—and learn what parents can do to help allay that fear.

PART TWO

Children's Concerns During the Breakup

2

Divorce Causes Separation Anxieties

"If Dad Left, Won't Mom Go Away Too?"

(Children's primary conflict created by the initial breakup is the fear of losing both their parents. Children are afraid that parental love won't be there when they need it and that their parents may even leave or abandon them. (This fear is not irrational when seen from the child's perspective; it is often based on their real-life experience. Usually without much preparation or warning, children suddenly see one of their parents pack his or her belongings and move away. Thereafter, the departing parent, usually the father, is often seen infrequently and irregularly.) This chapter examines how the threat of losing secure parental ties causes separation anxieties and many of the problems children experience in the aftermath of divorce.

The Causes of Children's Separation Anxieties

Why are three- to eight-year-old children so concerned about the permanence of their relationship with their parents? Shouldn't children who are well-adjusted before the divorce remain secure in their attachment to their parents? Most adults fail to appreciate the extent to which fear of abandonment exists in all children in early childhood. Even up to the age of eight or nine, most normal children have fears that their parents may leave them. Many children's fairy tales that have endured over the centuries reflect this concern. Hansel and Gretel, for example, were left in the woods. Cinderella's and Snow White's parents died, and both Little Red Riding Hood and Goldilocks were sent out into the forest alone. All children are afraid of being separated from their parents and not having anyone to care for them.

These normal fears of abandonment and loss are intensified by parental divorce. It seems to children that their worst fear is coming true—these all-important parents, the foundation of their universe, are going away. In effect, these children of divorce discover that relationships are not forever and that they can be left.

Thus the most common problem that the initial marital separation causes for young children is anxiety about separation and parental abandonment. Children experience these very painful feelings of separation anxiety for two reasons. First, these fears result from children's limited concept of time and their undeveloped thinking ability; second, they are caused by their attachment bonds and complete psychological and emotional dependence on parents.

Children's Limited Time Frame

A young child's perception of the world and sense of time is far more immediate and tied to the present than an adult's. Because of their limited thinking abilities, children have not yet learned how to project themselves hours and days into the future with the same certainty as adults. Thus when parents say, "I will see you in four days," children do not understand what this means and are not reassured about continuing contact. Or, for example, when parents leave children with a babysitter and go to the movies, young children cannot project ahead several hours and be secure in the knowledge that their mother or father will return. Underneath what appears to be a manipulative temper tantrum to keep mother or father at home may be a strong fear of being helpless and alone.

In addition, children's *object constancy* is still in an early stage of development. Object constancy begins as the recognition that an object still exists when it is removed from sight. Later, it is the security of understanding that a departing person will return. And, still later in development, object constancy becomes the capacity to be emotionally sustained by internal mental representations of loved ones and to feel psychologically connected to them in their absence. These complex cognitive and emotional achievements have not been fully attained by pre-school-aged children. And, for many older children and even adults in crisis, confidence in the constancy of relationships can still be shaken under the stress of intense emotional conflict.

This confidence can be easily upset when children are under the stress brought on by divorce because their object constancy has not yet become a stable cognitive ability. Before seeing what parents can do to help with this problem, we need to understand separation anxieties better by learning about attachment.

Attachment Bonds

The second and most important reason why children develop separation anxieties in response to their parent's breakup is because it threatens the security of their attachment bonds. To understand separation anxieties in children of divorce, we must first know something about the role of attachment in normal development.

Infants are biologically predisposed to form attachment bonds to their primary caretakers. Infants display this "attachment-seeking behavior" as early as the first two weeks of life. Babies prefer the human voice to other sounds, for example, and by four weeks prefer the mother's (the primary caretaker's) voice to that of others. At two months, they seek their mother's eyes and, to their mother's delight, hold this visual contact. At around three months, babies can recognize details in the human face sufficiently to discriminate human faces from other sights. Because infants' ability to recognize faces is such a great delight, they begin to smile at people at this time. If you think of the pleasure this smile provides parents, and the silly antics adults go through to elicit it, you begin to see how parents and children mutually attach to each other.

Between six and nine months, the infant's indiscriminate social smile becomes more selective. Attachment deepens and the child shows a strong preference for an inner circle of special caretakers. These attachment figures can elicit more delight than others, they can more readily comfort the infant in times of distress, and they create distress in the child when they leave. Researchers also have found that when infants have only their physical needs met but do not receive affection and attention from one or more consistent caretakers, they become depressed, apathetic, and retarded in their cognitive development. Simply put, humans need a warm, caring relationship in order to thrive and develop.

As toddlers, children use their primary caregivers as a secure base from which to venture out and explore the world. Thus, if parents have been emotionally responsive to children and comforting and available when needed, children will be securely attached. When tired, sick, or frightened, these securely attached children are reassured by knowing that they can return to their caregiver's lap for emotional refueling—and then they want to set off again to continue mastering the world. Paradoxically, rather than fostering the child's dependency, meeting these toddlers' dependency needs will later enable them to leave the caregiver more successfully and to confidently explore the environment on their own. Researchers find that securely attached infants become more effective problem solvers as toddlers, more enthusiastic and curious preschoolers, and more confident, independent school-aged children with higher self-esteem. In contrast, children feel insecurely attached when caregivers are inconsistently available or unresponsive to their distress or bids for attention. This lack of responsiveness often occurs because of parents' depression, fatigue, lack of interest, or preoccupation with their own problems.

The attachment bonds that, as children, we form with our parents are the essence of what is most human about us. Out of these early attachments develop our later capacities to feel empathy, compassion, and love for others. These attachments also form the basic building blocks of personality by giving us our most fundamental sense of whether we are lovable and whether we will find others trustworthy. Secure bonds are the greatest source of joy and contentment in childhood, but can also be the greatest source of anguish and despair when emotional ties are disrupted and caregivers are not available.

Attachment is not a one-way street; parents also form their own attachment bonds to young children. In many cases, these attachments will be the most intense and meaningful feelings that parents experience in their lives. These early caregiving years signal the love affair of a lifetime for many parents. When nonparents observe harried parents with tired eyes, stained shirts, and an armful of dirty diapers, they may wonder why anyone would choose to give up their freedom for such a life. These skeptical onlookers fail to see the powerful, loving bonds that often make this the most special time in life. Also, the later derivatives of these early attachment bonds make parents committed to their child's care and well-being for a lifetime. Let's look further now at how early attachment bonds carry over into later childhood and even adulthood, as well as how they can emerge as conflicts for divorcing parents.

ATTACHMENT BONDS CONTINUE THROUGHOUT LIFE. The nature of attachment bonds changes as children grow older, but these bonds continue to evolve throughout the lifespan. Older children become more independent and adolescents shift their ties from parents to peers. Even in adulthood, attachment does not wither, but remains a central, organizing force in intimate relationships. Throughout life, adults revisit attachment issues as intense love and anguish continue to go hand in hand. Enduring relationships hold the deepest satisfactions and yet leave us vulnerable to hurt, betrayal, and loss. Many divorcing parents, in particular, will struggle with the question of whether or not to risk involvement in another relationship. No pat answers can be given to such personal questions because the feelings involved are so profound, but as parents grieve and resolve the loss of the marriage, most of them will choose to love and commit again.

Attachment issues also come to the fore for divorcing parents in the intense ambivalence and distress they experience around the time of the initial separation, and these difficult feelings may last a year or two, or more, after the divorce. This lengthy recovery period occurs, in part, because the attachment bonds to the marital partner have been disrupted, but still have power, as revealed, for example, when divorced parents find themselves missing their former spouses, even though they are clear that the marriage was harmful to them and they truly want out. These parents genuinely do not want the marriage and so they are confused by their lingering feelings for their former spouses. At times, they may wonder if they really want to end the marriage and may begin a cycle of re-engaging, seeking sexual contact, and then distancing from their former spouses in a way that drives everyone crazy. This ambivalence is often just the gradual relinquishing of the attachment ties to the former spouse and has nothing to do with still being in love with the former spouse.

ATTACHMENT DISRUPTIONS IN YOUR LIFE. Let's look at another way to appreciate the importance of attachment bonds throughout childhood and adulthood. It is almost impossible for parents to fully appreciate children's complete physical and psychological dependence on them and the life-and-death intensity of children's attachment bonds. It is especially hard for parents to appreciate this continuing and intense need as preschoolers begin to push parents away and school-aged children act independent and self-assured by seven or eight. However, a closer look at our adult needs for continuing close relationships may help us to be more sensitive to children's attachment bonds and the separation anxieties that result from the breakup of their parents' marriages.

Get a pen and a piece of paper, and write down your answers to these three questions:

1. What was the most upsetting personal experience you have had in the last three years?
2. What was the most difficult and painful experience in your adult life?
3. What was the most traumatic experience of your childhood?

The answers most people give to all three questions will share a common theme. For men and women, and for each of the three age periods, most of the replies will involve the loss of a primary relationship. Examples commonly given are the death of a parent or loved one, the termination of a love relationship, or the loss of someone important who moved away. Even as adults, our greatest concerns are for the stability and continuity of close interpersonal relationships. Yet our dependency on and need for these attachments is far less than children's. This exercise should help us appreciate the intensity of the attachment needs of young children, which are primarily satisfied by the parents.

Children must be given secure attachment ties. Providing this "secure base" is the essential task of early parenting. To achieve this confidence, children must be certain of their ability to obtain their parent's attention and affection when they need it. When children cannot dependably elicit this attention and affection, the basic insecurity that results tends to remain a lifelong personality trait.

For many reasons, divorce all-too-often threatens or disrupts children's attachment bonds. Researchers have found that adults who grew up in divorced families are far more likely to report symptoms of insecure attachments than adults from intact homes. For example, adults who grew up in divorced homes were more likely to be bothered by crying spells, insomnia, constant worry, feelings of worthlessness or unlovability, guilt, and hopelessness. Decades later, these adults were also more likely to feel afraid, anxious, and angry when alone. These symptoms correspond to the feelings we call separation anxieties in young children who are distressed over separation from their attachment figures.

Thus the security of attachment ties will be central to children's short- and long-term adjustment to divorce. However, these attachment bonds need not be threatened by the divorce. Parents can do a great deal to ensure secure relational ties for their children in the aftermath of divorce. Before we go on to see what parents should and should not do, however, parents need to understand better when separation anxieties are occurring and why attachment ties are threatened by marital disruption.

How Marital Separation Threatens Children's Attachments

Separation anxieties may be the most painful feelings that children and adults experience in life. Much of the pain and conflict that three- to seven-year-old children experience as a result of divorce results from their anxiety about separation and abandonment. It must be stressed that whether or not children overtly communicate their fear of being left, divorcing parents should expect their children to have these fears.

When parents decide to divorce, the father usually moves out of the house and establishes a new residence for himself. The day of the move is almost always one of the most difficult times for the divorcing couple. The fact that the relationship is ending becomes a reality after months of just thinking and talking about it. Understandably, both spouses are caught up in their own feelings of anger, sadness, disbelief, numbness, or relief. At this moment, it's very likely that the parents' emotional reactions are so consuming that it's hard for them to pay attention to what their child is going through.

Try to imagine the thoughts and feelings a typical three- to seven-year-old child might have on the day that Dad leaves: "Mom and Dad have been crying and yelling a lot. They seem real unhappy. Mom said Dad was going to move today and he drove away in a big truck. Will I have to move, too? I don't want to go. I want Dad to come back. When will Dad be back? Is Mom going to move somewhere, too? She said that we would stay in our house and that I could keep my room, but Dad was leaving. If Dad went away, won't Mom go away, too? Maybe she'll drive away and leave me here all by myself. Maybe Mom and Dad are mad at me and don't want me anymore. I'm scared to be alone."

Virtually all young children will have some of these thoughts and feelings in response to their parents' separation. Divorcing parents need to anticipate that three- to ten-year-old children will become anxious because their security is threatened. Both young boys and girls will express this heightened sense of insecurity through increased bed-wetting, thumb-sucking, fear of the dark, nightmares, and clinging. These anxiety symptoms can develop into aggressive defiance or childhood depression if the feeling of insecurity isn't alleviated.

Because parents find the idea of deserting their children inconceivable, they often have difficulty understanding their children's separation anxieties and abandonment fears. These fears threaten all young children of divorce, and parents need to reassure children about the permanence of their relationship. Parents need to be alert to the ways children behave when they are frightened of being left on their own.

Divorcing parents can learn to recognize patterns of behavior that signal their children's separation anxieties or fear of being left. Children will start to have trouble with everyday partings that never bothered them before. Four-year-old Alicia, who bounded out of the car and eagerly ran to the nursery school playground before the divorce, now clings to her mother and cries as she tries to leave. Johnny, who used to be easy to put to bed at night, now exasperates his mother with endless requests for one more story, one more drink of water, or with fears that monsters will come if he is left alone in the dark. Or the arrival of the babysitter may trigger a temper tantrum that can ruin an evening out for even the most patient and guiltless parent. Any departure of the parent, even for a brief time, intensifies the child's fear of abandonment.

Adults usually respond to this kind of behavior with frustration and anger. This reaction is understandable, but unfortunately becomes part of a vicious circle that only exacerbates both the child's and the parent's conflicts. The frustrated parent often will become angry and threaten or punish the child. In response to this anger, the child will feel rejected and pushed away from the parent at the very moment when the need to feel close is intense. Consequently, children feel even more alone and afraid of being left, and their need for parental reassurance becomes even greater. The child's demanding behavior then escalates and further alienates the frustrated parent. If the parent does not understand the child's fear, life can become miserable for both of them.

Another situation that commonly stimulates children's separation anxieties is the weekly transition between the primary residence and the visit with the noncustodial parent. For example, I met the divorcing parents of a three-year-old girl who would talk all day about the fun she would have when she visited her father. On Wednesday her father always arrived to take her daughter home for the night, as per the visitation agreement. However, as soon as they began to leave the mother's home, the child would begin to cry, and she would remain upset for the rest of the evening. The next day the father would return her to her mother and, once again, the little girl would talk about her father and how she wanted to be with him.

How could these parents make sense of their daughter's contradictory behavior? Because their daughter was so reluctant to go with him, the mother was beginning to wonder whether her estranged husband was doing something terrible to the girl. In turn, the father felt rejected by the child and resentful of the mother because his daughter so obviously chose her over him. At the time I met them, he was becoming less interested in spending regularly scheduled time with his daughter.

After talking with the parents about children's separation anxieties, which are very strong in three-year-olds, the parents recognized that their daughter was going through this conflict. They realized that her distress over leaving her mother began exactly at the time the father moved out of the house. Once the parents understood that her father's original departure had aroused their daughter's fear of being left, I was able to help them talk with their child about her abandonment fears and explain more fully what the divorce meant. Both parents were able to reassure her that, even though they would be living in different houses, they would both always be her mother and father and they would never go away or leave her. Within the same week, the girl was able to make the transition from her mother's home to her father's without any trouble.

Explaining the Divorce to Your Children

Parental Explanations for the Initial Separation

Children are far more likely to develop abandonment fears and separation anxieties if they are not prepared for the parental separation. The entire divorce process will be much easier for children to cope with if they are told in advance what to expect. All too often children awaken one morning to find that their father is no longer living with them. With limited or no explanation, he is simply gone. Children are told only that their father moved out last night and that their parents are going to "get a divorce."

When a parent leaves a child suddenly and without warning, this shocking and traumatic event can generate frantic anxiety, even if the child has not been especially close to or involved with the departing parent. These children are going to experience strong separation anxieties; they do not know why their father has gone, what their future contact with him will be, or who else will leave.

Parents should tell children about the divorce when it is a firm decision. The best approach is for both parents to jointly talk with the children whenever such unity is possible, and it is usually better to tell children together, rather than separately, so that children can begin to comfort each other. It is critical that parents tell children a week or so in advance. If one parent moves out before they have been informed, the shock will always be highly distressing for children. When parents move apart, they should provide the child with frequent and predictable contact that begins immediately upon the parent's departure. If possible, the absent parent should try to visit or telephone the child every day for the first week or so. It is essential for children to know in advance specifically when and where they will visit their parent again. Visitation schedules should never be random, and parents must carefully follow through and strictly adhere to whatever schedule has been established. This predictability is vital.

As noted earlier, abandonment fears and separation anxieties are one of the greatest sources of emotional and behavioral problems in young children following divorce. The best way to prevent these symptoms from developing is to help children feel more control over their lives by preparing them for what is going to happen and by explaining why mother or father is moving away. Both mother and father, together if possible, should prepare their children by:

1. Telling them what to expect (that is, what is going to happen and when).
2. Providing an explanation for the divorce that the children can understand.
3. Reassuring the children of their permanent and continuing relationship with both parents.

Because children have a difficult time understanding what divorce means, parents often find it hard to explain. To help with this problem, this section offers suggestions on how to talk to your children about divorce. Sample parent–child dialogues are provided to illustrate how parents can alleviate separation anxieties and other concerns. I encourage you to rewrite and modify these scripts to make them more your own and to better fit your personal situation. The words can be spoken in a thousand different ways—the ideas are what is important.

1. *Tell children what to expect.* Parents should tell children that mother and father are going to get a divorce and will not be living together any more. Children should be told when the departing parent is going to move out and when they will be able to see him or her. Children should also be assured of continuing contact with both parents. Of course, it is not always possible to be so rational and controlled during the crisis of a marital breakup. However, it is important that parents exercise as much self-restraint and plan

as carefully as possible under these trying circumstances. How the breakup is handled initially with the children and the marital partner will have a significant bearing on the problems children will develop later and the couple's ability to cooperate in the years following the divorce.

As stated above, it is preferable for the mother and father to explain the divorce to their child together. This communicates to the child the all-important message that both parents will be working together and staying actively involved in the child's life. For example, in the sample dialogues that follow, mother and father alternately speak to their child:

> MOTHER: Daddy and I are not going to be married any more. We are going to get a divorce. We are going to live in different houses from now on, but we will still always be your Mommy and Daddy. That is never going to change.
>
> FATHER: I am going to move to a new place on Saturday morning. You are going to live here with Mommy, but you will be able to stay with me at my new home sometimes.
>
> MOTHER: You will live with me here, but Daddy will still want to be with you, too. We have arranged for you to be with him every _____ and you will also stay at his house on _____.
>
> FATHER: I will miss seeing you every day, but I'll look forward to having you with me on _____. I will talk to you on the phone on _____ between our visits.
>
> MOTHER: Even though Daddy and I are not going to be married any more, you will always live with one of us. We will both always love you and we will work together to take care of you until you are grown up.

2. *Provide an explanation for the divorce.* In addition to letting the child know what to expect, parents need to provide an explanation for why the divorce is occurring. Researchers have found that having an explanation for the divorce that they can understand is one of the best predictors of child adjustment after divorce. Incredibly, one significant study found that children were not given an explanation for their parents divorce eighty percent of the time. Parents do not talk with their children about divorce for a variety of reasons. Some simply feel that they don't know what to say. Others are afraid of making their child feel bad or of allowing their

own sadness or guilt to surface. But no matter how difficult it is to talk to children about an impending separation and divorce, it must be done. If parents find this step too difficult to take, they must seek professional help.

Let's look at one kind of parental "explanation" that commonly occurs, yet is not at all helpful to the child:

THERAPIST: How did you and your husband explain the divorce to your eight-year-old daughter, Lucy? Tell me exactly what you said to her.

MOTHER: Oh, we didn't really say much about it to her. She seemed to have figured it all out by herself.

THERAPIST: How do you know that?

MOTHER: Well, the day after my husband moved out, I overheard Lucy talking with the girl next door. Her friend asked if her daddy had moved away, and Lucy said, "Yeah, my parents are getting divorced." Since she seemed to know what was going on, I didn't see any point in saying anything more about it.

This kind of nonexplanation occurs frequently. If parents don't provide an explanation, children will create one of their own. As we will see in chapter 4, the explanations that children develop by themselves cause significant problems because children tend to blame themselves for the divorce (for example, "Dad moved out because he's mad at me"). Thus, even though it is difficult to talk to children about divorce, they adjust far better when they are given a clear and specific explanation.

One of the most difficult aspects of explaining divorce to children is dealing with the issue of blame. In many marital separations, one parent has initiated the breakup and the other spouse does not want the divorce. The spouse who has been left behind usually feels rejected, hurt, and angry, and often wants to enlist the children in blaming the departed spouse for breaking up the family. It is very troubling for the child when one parent assigns blame for the divorce and communicates that the child should also be angry with the parent who has left or should not want to be with him or her. Often this blame is assigned by inappropriately providing children with specific details of adult infidelities and sexual relationships. Although tempted to do so, parents should resist this impulse to tell the truth—or the truth as they see it—when this means creating good guys and bad guys and drawing children into competing alliances. This issue of blame is examined more fully in a later chapter.

The following explanation for the divorce should help children understand why their parents are parting, communicate that this is an adult decision and that the child is in no way responsible for the divorce, and prevent the alienation of the child from either parent.

> FATHER: We loved each other when we got married and when you were born, but we are not happy being married anymore.
>
> MOTHER: Sometimes parents' feelings about each other change as time goes by, and that is what has happened to us. We do not feel the same way as we used to about each other because we are both different now.
>
> FATHER: It's hard for us to get along with each other anymore because some things about Mommy make me unhappy, and some things about me make her unhappy. We have decided that we want to live apart from now on.
>
> MOTHER: We want you to know that the divorce is not your fault. There is nothing you could have done or can do about it. Divorce is a problem between the adults in the family; it is between Daddy and me.
>
> FATHER: Even though the way we feel about each other has changed, our love for you has not changed. We love you and are going to be working together to take care of you until you are grown up. Parents have a very special love for their children and that kind of love does not change. Parents and children never get a divorce.
>
> MOTHER: It is hard for Daddy and me to understand the problems between us, so I know that it is even harder for you to understand why we are getting a divorce. You can talk to us about the divorce whenever you want, and we will try and answer all of your questions.

3. *Reassure the children of their continuing relationship with both parents.* Even if young children are prepared for the marital separation and understand why it is happening, separation anxieties will still be aroused and they will feel insecure about the permanence of their relationship with their parents. Parents can alleviate children's painful separation anxieties, and the symptoms that accompany them, by repeatedly communicating that mother and father will always want to be with them and will never go away. One way of expressing this is suggested below.

Mommy/Daddy and I do not live together anymore. She/He has moved to a new home now. Maybe you have worried that since Mommy/Daddy and I do not want to live together any longer we might not want to live with you. Sometimes boys and girls worry about this when their parents get divorced. I want you to know that we do not feel that way. We will never leave you alone. Daddy/Mommy and I both love you and will always want to be with you. You will always live with one of us and we will always be here to take care of you.

This message will go a long way toward diminishing the fear of losing parental love that most children experience during the initial breakup. Parents should remember that their children will need to discuss these issues many times. Children will need to ask the same questions about the divorce—and receive the same reassurances—over and over again. Understandably, it will take many repetitions before children, especially young children, can trust these reassurances because the feelings involved are so profound and the stakes so high.

Explaining a Trial Separation

The previous dialogues address the situation in which mother and father have clearly decided to move apart and divorce. In many cases, however, there will be an extended period of uncertainty about the future of the marriage. One parent moves out, but the couple may continue spending time together and exploring the possibility of staying together. Such a trial separation can also affect children, and parents must consider how to present this ambiguous, transitional period to them.

Parents sometimes wonder, "Will it confuse the children if my spouse moves out but we continue to date?" Or, "Will it be harder for the children to accept the divorce if we have a trial separation first?" A trial separation is not necessarily better or worse for children than a complete break. Parents can decide to date each other, take a temporary time-out from the marriage, or go ahead and end the marriage, depending on their own wishes. The nature of the separation is less important to a child's adjustment than the way it is presented.

Many of the same guidelines for divorcing parents apply to trial separations, as well. Children should be prepared for the parental separation at least several days in advance. It is simply too threatening for children to wake up and find a parent gone or to see a parent move out after a fight. In addition, the absent parent and child should have regularly scheduled visits several times each week and telephone contact almost daily, beginning immediately following the departure. Children's primary fear is of losing access to the parent, and this can be assuaged by always knowing when and where they will see the out-of-home parent next.

Although children will be deeply concerned about a trial separation, they will be able to cope *if their emotional connection to both parents is maintained.* When children lose physical or emotional access to either parent separation anxieties and other significant symptoms become an enduring problem. The script below communicates these important reassurances while realistically presenting to the child what is going to happen and why. Of course, parents must not merely promise to remain with children or be supportive of the other parent's continuing relationship with children. Parents must follow through and reliably enact these reassurances for many years.

Daddy/Mommy and I are not happy living together right now. We are going to live apart for awhile so that we can decide whether we are going to stay married or get divorced. Mommy/Daddy is going to move into his/her own place for awhile. We will not know for several months if we are going to live together again or not, but we will let you know as soon as we decide. We want you to know that we are not unhappy with you, and we will never leave you or stop loving you.

While Mommy/Daddy and I are deciding whether we will stay married or get a divorce, you will be living with _____ at _____. Mommy/Daddy will still want to be with you, too, so we have arranged for you to visit with him/her every _____ and you will stay at his/her home on _____. You will also be able to talk with him/her on the telephone whenever you want to.

This is going to be a very big change for all of us. You will probably have a lot of questions to ask both of us after you have thought about this for a while. What questions can we try to answer for you right now?

The scripts I have suggested may not fit exactly with your personal circumstances. Some parents, for example, may be bitter and angry toward their spouses and may not plan to allow the other parent to spend time with the children. Or sometimes one parent is not interested in maintaining regular involvement with the children after divorce. These and other situations will be addressed in later chapters because they pose particular problems for children. For now, the point is that clear explanations such as these should be offered to ease the adjustment for children.

When Abuse Has Occurred

Perhaps the most important thing divorcing parents can do for their children is to honor and protect their relational ties to both parents. Children will be intensely concerned about their ability to sustain physical and emotional access to their parents, and it is essential for both parents to help children maintain secure attachments. All children have strong attachment needs and will become highly anxious (and later depressed) when they are uncertain of when and how they will be able to be close to both parents. This section, however, looks at one exception to the rule that parents must help children maintain ties. In a few circumstances, continuing ties expose children to physical, sexual, or emotional abuse. Although these painful topics are not relevant to most readers and are generally beyond the scope of this book, at times they are an aspect of divorce and must be addressed.

A few marriages break up because one parent is behaving irresponsibly toward a child and the other parent must protect the child from physical, sexual, or emotional abuse. In other families, abuse that has been occurring secretly may be uncovered during the period of crisis that often surrounds the initial breakup. Myths and misunderstandings are pervasive in this highly disturbing area of abuse. Furthermore, although everyone wants to turn away from this painful topic, we can protect children better by not avoiding it.

Who commits sexual abuse? By a factor of five, the most common perpetrator is a stepfather. One typical scenario is that in which the mother was molested as a child, has not worked through this trauma with professional help, and is still unaware of or denies what happened to her. Remarkably, the stepfather often molests his stepdaughter when she is the same age as the mother was when she was molested. When fathers molest children, alcoholism is usually an accompanying symptom. Perhaps the most disturbing fact about child sexual abuse is that in three-fourths of all cases the perpetrator knows the child well and is a family member, close family friend, or member of the extended family. Thus, violation of trust is one of the most essential characteristics of sexual abuse.

Which children are most vulnerable? A common misconception about child sexual abuse is the Lolita myth. Many people believe that the sexually developing, precocious adolescent is most at risk; however, in fact, teenagers are more assertive and can say no more effectively. As a result, molestation seldom begins in adolescence. Instead, the child most likely to be molested is a five- to seven-year-old girl. She is also most likely to be a victim if she is depressed, excessively compliant, and receiving too little affection and attention. Boys are sexually molested as well, but the incidence is about twice as high for girls.

How can parents know if their children are being abused? Young children will re-enact with dolls or in their drawings and play what has been done to them. Parents should pay close attention whenever children make such drawings or use dolls in sexually explicit play. If this type of play occurs, children are often acting out inappropriate adult–child contact that they have experienced. Similarly, whenever children tell parents about sexual contact with an adult, or communicate that they must keep a "secret," parents must never dismiss these concerns. Rather parents must explore these statements further in order to protect their children. Parents can do this by contacting their pediatrician or family practice physician for further assessment.

Myths and denial also surround physical abuse. As with sexual abuse, the biggest problem is that adults/caretakers do not want to believe that this abuse could actually be occurring and tend to ignore the signs. The person most likely to physically abuse a child is a mother, and the most likely victim is either an early adolescent or a very young child under two years of age.

Physical abuse is equally likely for boys or girls, and almost always takes place while the parent is trying to discipline the child. Physically abusing families tend to be socially isolated and, in general, tend to be highly authoritarian (that is, cold and very strict) in their child-rearing. When parents see unexplained marks or bruises on a child, physical abuse may be the cause. Parents should neither overreact and make accusations nor ignore these signs and assume that nothing is wrong. Again, a responsible first step is to have your child examined immediately by your family pediatrician.

Do parents sometimes make false allegations of physical and sexual abuse to intimidate the former spouse during heated divorce proceedings? Yes, unfortunately. Do parents sometimes ignore legitimate signs of abuse, fail to protect their children, and feel terribly guilty later? Yes, unfortunately. In cases in which sexual or physical abuse is occurring, limits must be placed on the child's contact with the abusing parent—for example, by requiring that visits with the child be supervised at all times. Parents coping with these extenuating circumstances need to seek additional psychological help for themselves and their children.

The most frequent form of abuse is emotional. Again, although continuing close contact with both parents is usually one of the most important reassurances that divorcing parents can offer children, there are important exceptions. For example, researchers have found that young adults who were children of divorce find it especially difficult to achieve in school or work or to establish satisfying love relationships when one parent has been derogating or undermining.

Although embattled parents are usually very reluctant to acknowledge this fact, children are emotionally abused when they are repeatedly exposed to parental fights. It is profoundly upsetting for children when their parents continually threaten and fight in front of them or embroil children in their battles. Combative parents emotionally abuse their children by making them take sides, carry messages back and forth, or by blaming children and making them feel responsible for marital conflicts.

During the chaotic initial phase of breaking up, parents often respond to each other, and sometimes to their children, in emotionally abusive ways. The consequences endure for a lifetime for children whose parents repeatedly yell at them in hatred or disgust or tell them that they are stupid, worthless, or bad. If parents find that they have lost control of themselves and said hurtful things like this, they should apologize to their children, tell them it is not true, and acknowledge making a mistake. Such parents should also seek help in counseling. Sadly, these parents are almost always saying exactly the same hurtful words to their children that their own parents once said to them.

The primary concern in divorcing families, however, is the emotional abuse of children that occurs when parents lose control and cannot stop fighting with each other. Researchers have found that boys, more than girls, are especially likely to suffer lifelong insecurities from chronic marital conflict. Although physical and sexual abuse will not be a concern for most divorcing couples, emotional abuse of children through chronic marital conflict is prevalent. Throughout this book, I stress the very serious problems that befall children when parents do not shield them from ongoing parental battles and suggest what parents can do to help with this problem. For now, however, the main point is that children's unprotected involvement with sexually, physically, or emotionally abusive parents engenders anxiety and shame rather than security.

In most cases, however, parents need to reassure children that their all-important bonds to both parents will remain constant. This reassurance can help alleviate the single biggest concern that divorce arouses for young children—the fear of losing their parents.

The next chapter turns to a second cause of problems for many children during the initial stage of breakup: reunification fantasies.

3

Children Want to Reunite Their Parents

"If I'm Really Good, Maybe Mom and Dad Will Get Back Together Again."

We have just seen in chapter 2 that children become anxious when their parents break up. One way children cope with this anxiety-arousing loss is to deny the reality of the divorce and try to keep their parents together. Although one or both of the parents may want the divorce, children do not. Thus, children initially deny what is occurring and try to figure out what they can do to keep their parents together. Although they may not talk about it openly, many children tenaciously hold onto this desire to recreate the original family structure for many years after the divorce. The reunification wish is often so strong that it continues even after one or both parents have remarried and given birth to new children. Similarly, the hope remains despite the realization that the divorce has resulted in less fighting at home and a better life for everyone in the family. Children simply do not want to accept the fact that the marital relationship has ended.

Reunification fantasies are not just benign childhood wishes. They prevent children from coming to terms with the reality of their current life and from successfully moving forward in their development. If parents do not give definitive explanations for the divorce that end these reunification fantasies, they can cause problems for years afterward. Once parents have decided they are going to divorce, they must tell children that the divorce is final and that the children can do nothing to change that fact. Of course, this can be excruciating for parents to say. And—to make things harder—parents should anticipate that this statement will be as hard for children to hear as it is for parents to speak. Explanations about the permanence of the breakup are necessary, however, and they help children cope more effectively in the long run. Children will not be able to adjust to the new circumstances of their lives until they are certain that their mother and father will never be married again.

Three Sources of Reunification Fantasies

Why do most school-aged children cling to the hope that their mothers and fathers will not divorce or that they will eventually remarry? Why do some children even develop symptoms of illness or other behavior problems in order to get their parents back together? Reunification fantasies can stem from three different sources, each of which has a very different meaning for children and requires a different parental response.

First, children want to avoid the painful feelings caused by the breakup. They want to maintain their family as they have known it and to believe that their parents love and are happy with each other. This response to the initial breakup is almost universal. This first source of reunification fantasies does not tend to cause long-term problems for children, especially if parents provide explanations for the divorce that clearly communicate its finality.

The second source of reunification fantasies is very different and far more problematic for children. In some families, an effective parental coalition has never formed, so that the children have learned that they can effectively come between their parents and manipulate the closeness in their parent's marriage. These children, who are often demanding and difficult to discipline, have been too successful in controlling family relations before the divorce. With the divorce, they often develop further problems as they try to manipulate adult relationships and keep their parents together.

The third and most serious source of reunification fantasies is when one parent does not want the divorce and enlists the child in convincing the other parent to remain married. Each of these three types of reunification fantasies deserves more detailed examination.

Normal Reunification Fantasies

Normal, or expectable, reunification fantasies are the most common and the least problematic for children. They are also the easiest for parents to resolve. Such fantasies can occur for several reasons.

Perhaps the simplest reason why some children think their parents will reconcile is because they have seen this happen. Often children have heard their parents threaten to separate, but these threats have never before come true. Furthermore, many children have witnessed several temporary marital separations. It makes sense for these children to think that the latest separation can be reversed, too.

Children also develop unrealistic reunification fantasies in order to deny the reality of the initial breakup. It is too painful to acknowledge that the separation is real all at once, so children (and adults) often cope by gradually accepting the reality.

Much of the pain that children avoid springs from the loss of the intact family and the protection and familiarity it provides. Children have a strong need for their parents to be happy and affectionate together, and as long as they stay together, children feel more secure. In the previous intact family, children were also part of a larger family group that gave them their own place in the world and the sense of belonging that comes from family membership. Even though there may have been tension and conflict before the divorce, the intact family still offered the security of familiarity. In contrast, after the divorce the family structure will be anxiety-arousing for children just because it is new and unknown.

Children's reunification fantasies are also fueled by a heightened insecurity about having their basic needs met. Although children's dependency increase during divorce, they do not feel as confident that they can rely upon their parents to fulfill those needs. Insecurity is further increased because relationships do not seem as stable or as permanent as they did before the breakup. This anxiety is exacerbated because children usually find that they have far less contact with their fathers after the separation. And, when children see their parents' distress over the breakup, the myth that parents are totally in control of life also ends. Perhaps for the first time, children become aware that their all-important and all-powerful parents have their own needs, concerns, vulnerabilities, and limitations.

For all of these reasons, children do not want to accept that the divorce is permanent and instead hold onto the fantasy that their parents will reunite. As noted before, however, this is not just a harmless childhood wish. Children use reunification fantasies to ward off painful feelings of loss and sadness at the ending of the family as they have known it. This denial prevents children from accepting the reality of the divorce and moving forward to adapt to their new family life. Parents can help children end these encumbering reunification wishes, as discussed at the end of this chapter.

Children's Manipulation of the Parental Coalition

In order to understand the second source of reunification fantasies, we must first turn to the topic of "structural family relations" and learn some concepts from family systems theory. Structural family relations is a term used to describe the basis for family organization and to define how the family operates as a social system. This term refers to the relatively enduring patterns of alliances, coalitions, loyalties, and alignments that exist in every family. Structural family relationships shape family communication patterns and the roles that family members adopt. Among the different structural family relationships, the parental coalition is the pivotal axis of family life and shapes much of how the family functions. In particular, the nature of the parental coalition primarily determines how well children adjust. This fact is just as true for divorced families as it is for intact families and, as we will see in chapter 11, it applies to stepfamilies as well.

In intact families that function well, the marital relationship is the primary two-person relationship in the family. Both spouses have a loyal commitment to each other so that the marital coalition cannot be divided by their parents, children, friends, employers, or others. Parents in such a coalition will still have differences and conflicts between themselves, and they will be committed to others as well, but their marital relationship is a stable alliance that cannot be disrupted by others. However, in some families the primary emotional bond or involvement is not between mother and father, and the children of these families often struggle with enduring personality conflicts. In these more problematic families, the primary alliance is between a grandparent and parent, a parent and a child, or within some other dyad. If parents have been unable to form a primary marital coalition during courtship and early marriage, or have lost it during the stressful period of early child-rearing, divorce is far more likely.

Another element in the structure of family relationships is how children try to manipulate closeness in their parents' marriage. Children's response to closeness in their parents' relationship is paradoxical. On the one hand, when parents are physically and emotionally close, children often will try to get between them and separate them. On the other hand, when parents separate and divorce, children often will try to reunite them.

Parents may observe that, as early as the age of two, children will consistently try to come between them. For example, toddlers will physically separate their parents by climbing between them when they sit down together. Three-year-olds command their fathers, "Don't talk to my Mommy". Four-year-olds may direct parents to stop kissing. Older children often interrupt, talk loudly, or become a nuisance when mother and father try to talk together. Children will also attempt to play one parent off against the other or try to get one of their parents to side with them against the other parent.

In these ways, children test the limits of their ability to come between their mother and father. Rather than accepting the existing primary relationship between spouses, they attempt to redefine the primary relationship as the one between themselves and one parent. If parents are unable to maintain their fundamental relationship as a couple and their alliance is disrupted, children will have more problems. This type of disruption in the structure of family relations can greatly exacerbate reunification fantasies.

As we have seen, one of the most important dimensions of family life is whether children are successful in disrupting the marital coalition between parents. If children repeatedly succeed in coming between the mother and father, problems develop because children exert more control over parental relationships than is healthy for them or the family. If their parents divorce, children who could push their parents apart will naturally feel that they also have the power to bring them back together. It seems possible to these children that they can reunite their parents because they have already learned that they can influence the closeness in their parents' marital relationship.

In contrast, in healthy families that function well, parents are able to maintain their emotional alliance with each other and children learn that they cannot come between their parents or manipulate the closeness in their relationship. The parents are in charge of family relationships, not the children. As a result, if parents with a successful marital coalition divorce, their children will not be likely to develop this second and more serious type of reunification fantasy. Because they have not been able to manipulate parental relationships before the divorce, children will be less likely to develop problems that are disguised attempts to get their parents back together.

Later chapters will examine how parents can work together to establish a successful parental coalition after the divorce even though they couldn't achieve one during the marriage. For now, however, consider a family in which the child has been able to disrupt the marital alliance.

Charles and his wife Eva had grown apart over the past few years. They couldn't relate to one another the way they used to, and although Charles didn't quite understand why, it seemed that something always prevented them from being close.

On their tenth wedding anniversary, however, Charles was determined to make the night different, so he was taking Eva to her favorite restaurant. Charles had bought a beautiful gold watch and had it engraved as a present for her. He wanted this night to be romantic for the two of them.

Charles and Eva were both excited as they showered and dressed. They were anticipating a lovely evening ahead—something they hadn't shared in a long time. Charles finished dressing first and went downstairs to get their five-year-old son, Adrian, ready for bed.

"Hey, Adrian, why don't you put your pajamas on early so you'll be all ready for Mrs. Aames when she gets here?"

"I don't want her to take care of me," Adrian whined. "She's mean and I'm not going to stay with her."

Charles was not in the mood for this kind of behavior and a loud argument quickly ensued. By the time Eva heard all the commotion and came downstairs, Adrian was already having a full-fledged temper tantrum and Charles was threatening to give him a spanking. Adrian rushed to his mother for comfort.

"What's the matter, Adrian? Tell me what's wrong."

"I hate Mrs. Aames," Adrian sobbed. "I don't want her to stay with me. I want another babysitter. Will you stay home with me?"

Charles was furious. "You *are* staying with Mrs. Aames tonight and your mother and I are going out. That's the final decision, period, end of discussion!"

"Now wait a minute, Charles," Eva said. "If Adrian really doesn't want to stay with Mrs. Aames, there must be a good reason. We can't just leave him when he's so upset. I'll read him a story and try to put him to bed early. Maybe we can go out a little bit later after he's fallen asleep."

Charles felt undermined by his son and betrayed by his wife. Something like this happened every time he tried to do something alone with his wife. As he looked at his wife holding their son, Charles felt angry, confused, and alone. Speaking slowly and deliberately, he replied, "Fine. The two of you have a wonderful evening together. I'm going out."

As he backed out of the driveway, Charles wondered whether he could return the watch.

CHILDREN DEVELOP PROBLEMS TO REUNITE THEIR PARENTS. Some of the problems children develop after their parents' divorce are actually veiled attempts to reunite their parents. Sometimes children will steal, fight, fail their classes, or become physically ill in response to parental separation. Especially in families without a stable marital coalition, children have learned that mother and father may come together to pursue the common goal of correcting their child's deviant behavior. By making trouble the child often succeeds in reuniting the parents—at least temporarily.

If the child is in trouble, the family alliances shift away from the parent–child union and the mother and father become a working team again. This process commonly occurs in families where the mother and father have repeatedly allowed the child to come between them and disrupt their marital relationship. The case of Charles, Eva, and Adrian is an example of how this process works and why it is harmful.

Three years later, Charles and Eva divorced. During the three years, Charles had become increasingly distant and unavailable, and Eva had become more attentive to and involved with Adrian than ever. When the separation finally happened, however, Adrian was terribly upset and became a behavior problem at school. His third-grade teacher reported that Adrian was not getting along with other children his age and was failing academically. As they had in the past, Charles and Eva came together to meet with school officials to discuss Adrian's behavior.

Like most children, Adrian did not want his parents to divorce and he wanted them to get back together. During the time leading up to the divorce, Adrian had learned that if he got into trouble at school his parents always responded as a team. His poor behavior precipitated those rare moments in the marriage when his parents would talk together and show mutual concern. Adrian felt that if he continued to get into trouble at school, his parents would have to stay together to work on his problems.

When the school counselor suggested to Charles and Eva that Adrian's behavior might be related to the divorce, that reasoning made sense to them. Yet, when the counselor also suggested that Adrian's problems were an attempt to reunite his parents, Charles thought the counselor was deluded. "How can you sit there and say Adrian's getting in trouble to keep us together when he's the one who's always come between us!"

Eva and Charles spent several more sessions with the school counselor. They talked in more detail about how children paradoxically try to come between their parents and interfere with their relationship when they are together and then try to reunite them when they part. Once both parents clearly understood that they had allowed Adrian to separate them when they were married, it was easier for the counselor to convince them not to let Adrian influence their relationship after the divorce.

With the school counselor's help, Charles and Eva spent a great deal of time and effort telling Adrian that the divorce was final and that he could do nothing to change that. Gradually, Adrian began to realize that his parents were probably telling him the truth. As he came to accept that the divorce was permanent, and that he could not do anything to get his parents back together again, Adrian's behavior problems at school began to diminish.

CONVINCING CHILDREN THAT THE DIVORCE IS FINAL. Obviously, reunification fantasies are not good for children and should be discouraged. The child's belief that mother and father will remarry is a denial of the reality of the divorce to ward off the inevitable and painful feelings associated with it. If this unwillingness to accept the divorce continues, children cannot move forward and adapt to their new family life.

However, this reluctance to accept reality raises serious concerns when children have learned to manipulate the closeness in the parental relationship. Such children are prone to intense reunification fantasies that endure for years or even decades. A more important consequence, however, is that children often develop problems in their attempt to reunite their parents. By developing these problems, children with sustained reunification fantasies are attempting to reconcile their parents at the expense of their own emotional well-being.

Children should not be allowed to manipulate adult relationships, either in intact or divorced families. The parents of children who want to influence their relationship must try to prevent their children from coming between them. For divorcing parents, a first step in resolving this situation is for both parents together to sit down and explain the divorce to their children. This joint action is one way to begin showing children that their parents are in charge and working together to take care of them. As stressed throughout this book, *the nature of the parental coalition and parents' ability to cooperate together are the most important determinants of children's adjustment to divorce.*

As with Charles and Eva, parents must clearly explain to children that their decision to divorce is irrevocable. Usually this discussion is very difficult for parents, and, as a result, they often avoid the topic. However, researchers have found that children who were given a full explanation of their parents' divorce that included the finality of the decision were better adjusted two years after the divorce than children who were not given this explanation. Several ways to discuss the divorce with children are suggested at the end of this chapter.

When One Parent Encourages the Reunification Fantasy

Although most school-aged children will try to stop their parents from separating and, years after the divorce, may still secretly harbor reunification fantasies, in one particular family situation, these fantasies are especially problematic. In some families, children's reunification fantasies are actively encouraged by the parent who has been left. Children caught in this situation are almost certain to develop serious emotional problems.

I first learned about these additional problems from an eight-year-old boy I'll call Johnny. Johnny's mother called the clinic to get help for her son. She reported that he was refusing to go to school, talking back to her rudely, and becoming unmanageable at home.

It became clear during the first counseling session that Johnny was convinced his parents were going to get back together. Johnny held this reunification fantasy even though his parents had been separated for several months and his mother was filing for divorce. I asked Johnny's mother if there were any possibility of a reconciliation between her and her husband, and she said no. I asked the mother to say that directly to Johnny. As she began to tell Johnny this, he jumped up onto the coffee table and announced that he was a powerful magician who knew that his mother and father were going to get married again. Johnny became very agitated as he stood on the coffee table; he gestured dramatically and proclaimed that his "magical powers" could make his parents get back together. It was sad to see this young boy making such a desperate attempt to take control.

At that time I couldn't understand why Johnny's reunification fantasy was so strong. Why did he embrace this reconciliation wish so completely that he was driven to conjuring up magical powers? The answer became clear when I asked Johnny's father to join us the following week to talk about the inevitability of the divorce with Johnny.

In that session I asked Johnny's father to tell him that his parents were going to get a divorce and that, although Johnny might not have wanted it to happen, there was nothing he could do to change it. The father stammered for a while and finally delivered a vague, watered-down version of what I had suggested. It was easy for Johnny to dismiss such a half-hearted explanation. Only then did it become clear to me that Johnny's father was the one who did not want to give up the reunification fantasy. The divorce had been his mother's decision and his father was using Johnny as a vehicle to prevent it. As the story gradually unfolded, it became clear that his father had been telling Johnny that he and his mother were very likely to stay married and that Johnny could help make them stay together.

I worked with Johnny's father to get him to accept that the divorce was inevitable. Finally, for the first time, the father began to share the sadness and disappointment that the divorce held for him. Only after he could start to deal directly with his own feelings did he stop encouraging Johnny's reunification fantasies and the inappropriate belief that Johnny had the power to control his parents' marriage. Before long, his father was able to tell Johnny convincingly that the divorce would happen and that Johnny could not change that fact. Although this news made Johnny sad, he also looked visibly relieved, and his symptoms diminished immediately. In a six-month follow-up conversation, I was told that Johnny was doing well in school and obeying his mother better at home.

Children should not be led to think that they can manipulate or control adult decisions to marry, divorce, have children, and so forth. As a result of this false belief, Johnny developed an unrealistic sense of his own power and control. As the "powerful magician," he tried to control his mother and make her remarry his father, but he was also terribly anxious over the prospect of having so much responsibility for his parents. Why did this power make Johnny so anxious and cause him to develop the problems he was having?

First, at eight, Johnny was far from grown up, and he still had many needs that could only be met by older and stronger adults. He accurately sensed that he could not entrust these needs to adults who could be manipulated or controlled by a child like himself. Children like Johnny are thus in a very difficult position: they have to act like adults while still needing to be taken care of as children. Johnny felt more secure and behaved accordingly when he could return to being just an eight-year-old boy. As such, he could depend on stronger adults to take care of him, rather than having to be responsible for them.

Second, we have already seen that children hold onto reunification fantasies as a way of avoiding their own painful feelings about the divorce. However, if one parent supports or fosters a child's fantasies about parental reunification, that child is very likely to develop personality or emotional problems. This use of the child to achieve what the parent cannot—reconciliation—is one example of a larger pattern wherein parents use their children to communicate with each other. When children are used as pawns in parental battles, the effective parental coalition that characterizes healthy family functioning does not occur. In intact, shared-custody, single-parent, or step-families that function well, children are not triangulated into adult interactions in this way and there is a clear division between adult business and child business. In subsequent chapters we examine in detail the highly significant problems that result when parents violate intergenerational boundaries and draw children into adult conflicts.

Explaining the Permanence of Divorce to Children

This chapter emphasizes the crucial need for parents to explain to their children that their decision to divorce is unalterable. In order to help children understand that the marriage is truly over, parents need to:

1. Make it absolutely clear that the decision to divorce is final and that the child can do nothing to change it.
2. Explain that there is no possibility whatsoever that Mom and Dad are going to reunite or remarry each other in the future.
3. Point out that the decision to divorce is strictly an adult decision and that children cannot change it because it is not their decision to make.

One effective technique to use in explanations to the child is to emphasize the difference—or boundary—between parents and children. This can be done by making a distinction between matters that concern only adults (buying a house, changing jobs, getting a new car, having another child) and matters that concern children as well as adults (family outings, family vacations, having pets, visiting school friends, assigning household chores). In the first instance, these issues and decisions do not directly involve children and cannot be influenced by them in any significant way; in the second, the issues involve discussion and input from each member of the family. Divorce is one of the adult issues that children have no control over or responsibility for.

Some specific ways that parents can use to talk with their children about their reunification fantasies—and help put them to rest—are suggested in the following sample dialogue.

MOTHER/FATHER: You've told me that you wish Daddy/Mommy and I would stay married so that all of us can live together again. I know that sometimes you wish we could have our old family back just the way it was, but I want you to know that cannot happen. Our decision to divorce is final and we are not going to change it.

CHILD: Well, maybe you'll change your mind later and want Daddy/Mommy to live with us again.

MOTHER/FATHER: I know you would really like it if Mommy/Daddy and I would stay married. But I want you to understand that our decision to divorce has been made. It is final, and that is not going to change. Sometimes when you feel bad about the divorce you can talk about it with Daddy/Mommy or me. But we are not going to change our minds and we are not going to be living together any more.

Or, an alternative script might be:

MOTHER/FATHER: Sometimes children believe that if they are really bad and get in trouble, or if they are really good all the time, it will help bring their parents back together again. That won't happen because your mother/father and I don't want to be together anymore. As much as you would like for us to stay married, there's nothing you can do to bring us back together. Divorce is strictly an adult decision made by your mother/father and me, and we are not going to be together again.

It is terribly difficult for parents to address their divorce so directly and so bluntly end their children's wishes to reunite the family. These words will be as painful for parents to say as they will be for children to hear. Parents must be prepared for their own sadness and guilt so that they can respond to the disappointment and anger this will arouse in their children. However, even though these conversations are hard to hold, parents and children alike will adjust better if these topics that everyone wants to avoid can be talked about and shared. Divorcing parents are working together in their children's best interest when they eschew blame, keep children out of parental conflicts, and provide needed explanations such as these.

4

Children Feel Responsible for the Divorce

"Maybe If I Had Been Good, Mom and Dad Wouldn't Have Gotten a Divorce."

Many children feel responsible and blame themselves for their parents' divorce. It's often hard for parents to imagine that their children could hold such a wildly mistaken belief, but many children do. Most children are firmly convinced that they have caused the divorce and that the breakup is all their fault. Whenever I am working with children of divorce I ask them if they caused their parents to divorce. The majority of children answer yes. I then ask them what they did that caused their parents to divorce. Their answers are always the same: a variation on the theme that they were somehow bad. For example, children regularly tell me, with great seriousness and conviction, that their parents divorced because "I didn't mind my dad enough," or because "my brother and I fought all the time," or because "I wasn't good." Such self-blame can continue in children for years after the divorce and can be the source of needless guilt and fears of reprisal.

Parents should expect this reaction and try to dispel this misconception. Fortunately, children's false assumption of responsibility can be eliminated through parental explanations and reassurances. Children can be greatly relieved to hear that their perception of their role in the divorce is not true and that they are in no way responsible. This chapter shows how parents can bring the issue of blame out into the open and explain to children that they are never responsible for adult decisions such as divorce. In line with explanations for the divorce, parents can explain that divorce is an adult decision—not child business. By helping children understand that the divorce is beyond their control, parents can address this false belief and lift the unnecessary burden of guilt and blame that many children carry.

Why Children Feel Responsible

There are several reasons why most children up to ten or twelve years of age believe they are to blame for the divorce. First, children are egocentric in their thinking—that is, they believe that the world revolves around them. In children's eyes, everything that goes on in the world is happening specifically to them or is caused by them. Furthermore, because of their cognitive immaturity and lack of intellectual development, very young children do not have a clear understanding of cause-and-effect relationships. For example, toddlers and preschoolers do not recognize that other people make decisions that affect them and yet are based on motives that have nothing to do with them. Because young children are highly egocentric in their thinking, they will experience life as if they are the center of the universe.

As children grow out of early childhood and into the early school years, this self-centered, egocentric thinking is increasingly replaced with a more realistic understanding of the world. Gradually, both the individuality of others and the nature of cause-and-effect relationships are grasped. However, as with the related concept of "magical" thinking discussed in chapter 3, the predisposition to consider oneself the cause of events still lingers, even through adolescence and adulthood. Adults' tendency to return to this egocentric mode of thinking is greatly increased in emotionally charged situations. For example, on being told that they have a medical emergency, adults can irrationally feel that they have been singled out to receive this punishment for some sin, defect, or inadequacy in themselves. Although it doesn't make sense, the belief that "I am responsible for this trauma and I am being punished" comes to the surface. However, while adults may temporarily revert to this unrealistic egocentric thinking when they are in crisis, children routinely think in this self-centered way. As a result, children feel responsible for events they have no control over, such as the death of a parent or marital disruption.

Other factors also make children feel responsible for their parents' divorce. All children get angry with their parents at times and wish they were dead, would go away, or would be replaced by other idealized parents. Children interpret these commonplace feelings as explanations for how they caused their parents' divorce. When parents divorce the child's wish that mom or dad would leave has come true. Naturally, it is frightening for children to believe that their angry thoughts have caused this to happen. Let's return to the concept of "magical" thinking and examine it further.

Magical thinking comes about because children do not fully understand the distinction between fantasy and reality. Parents can often observe their young children trying to discern between their thought and actions or asking whether something is "pretend or real." Many children worry and feel guilty because they believe that their "bad" wishes or feelings have caused the divorce. Understandably, children with this idea become afraid of their own destructive power. Imagine how alarming it would be if one's thoughts or emotions could control adult lives, send parents away, and destroy family relationships. Fortunately, this distorted concept of what has happened, and its accompanying sense of responsibility and blame, can easily be corrected by reassuring explanations from adults.

However, because these ideas are irrational and unimaginable to most adults, many parents never think of asking their children whether they think they caused the divorce. A few children will tell one parent that they think they caused the other parent to leave and will apologize for it. In most cases, though, children keep the secret of their blame to themselves. Nevertheless, if you ask your children directly if they have ever felt bad because they caused the divorce, the majority of four- to ten-year-old children will say yes. Many older children and adolescents also share this false belief to a lesser extent. By asking directly about their feelings of responsibility and self-blame, however, parents can offer children a more realistic explanation of the divorce and reassure them that they are blameless.

When Parents Blame Children

As we have seen, almost all children suffer from feelings of responsibility for causing their parent's breakup. In a few cases, however, parents also believe that their child is responsible for the divorce. In this minority of families, one or both parents tell children that they are responsible for the parental divorce. These parents say to their child:

"We broke up because of you."
"None of this would have happened if it weren't for you."
"I left your father/mother because of you."
"The divorce is your fault."

It is always a mistake to blame children in this way. When children are overtly blamed, their fear of being responsible is confirmed rather than assuaged by the parent, and such children will almost certainly develop substantial and enduring problems. In reality, of course, children are never responsible for adult decisions and must not be made to feel they are. When adults wish to avoid responsibility for their own decisions and actions, however, it is easy to shift this burden onto children. These parents may exclaim, "It's not my fault the marriage didn't work. Jimmy caused all the trouble. He wouldn't mind us and caused so many problems for us that we couldn't have a peaceful home. My husband couldn't stand it and left. Quite frankly, I don't really blame him."

Children, of course, never control such adult decisions. Parents who have told their children that the divorce was their fault must take back this responsibility and correct this mistake by simply telling their children that their accusations are not true.

Although many readers may find it hard to believe that parents could accuse their children in this way, such blame occurs regularly. The result is feelings of self-hatred and worthlessness in children that are often masked by chronic depression. More commonly, however, parents eschew responsibility in more subtle ways. For example, some parents shift responsibility onto the children by telling them that the divorce was undertaken in the child's best interest. These parents might say "I thought it would be best for you, Mary, if I left your father." Although far more subtle than overtly blaming the child, such statements again leave the child feeling responsible for something she did not want and had no control over. Whether the child is blamed directly or indirectly, the adult's feelings of failure, inadequacy, or guilt for the divorce are alleviated at the expense of the child. Children who are blamed overtly will believe that they are inherently bad. Those blamed more subtly feel guilty, develop a grandiose sense of their own omnipotence, and become anxious about the excessive control over others that they can seemingly exert.

Children and parents alike will adjust far better if parents can reclaim responsibility for their own decisions. This may be hard for some parents to do, but it is the only way to effectively take control of one's life. A realistic and satisfying feeling of personal power follows when one takes responsibility for one's own decisions. In most cases, parents who blame their children for the divorce are too afraid to admit that they have made a mistake. Rather than feeling merely that the marriage has failed, such parents often fear that the divorce confirms their sense of themselves as failures. These painful, exaggerated feelings of failure, which parents try to ward off by shifting the responsibility onto their children, were often fostered by their own parents' excessive criticism of them whenever they made mistakes as youngsters. In many cases, these blaming parents were brought up to believe they had to be perfect. As a result of this belief, they may feel unrealistically guilty about hurting their child, disappointing others, or failing to live up to religious mores.

Divorce does not necessarily demonstrate failure. In many situations it is a healthy and courageous step forward. However, even though they may feel like failures in the short run, divorcing parents who blame their children need to be more forgiving of themselves and allow themselves to have some setbacks. The true measure of people is not how often they stumble or make mistakes, but how they recover afterward. Parents who can be more accepting of themselves will not need to shift responsibility for the divorce onto their children. It is important for those who continue to feel that their child is to blame to explore this idea carefully with a therapist.

Guidelines for Talking with Children about the Divorce

Sample Scripts for Alleviating Blame

For the majority of families, parents simply need to provide children with an explanation that communicates they were in no way responsible for the divorce. Several suggestions on how to put this message into words follow.

> MOTHER/FATHER: Sometimes when mothers and fathers decide they are going to divorce each other, their children think that they caused the divorce. Have you ever had any thoughts like that?
>
> CHILD: No.
>
> MOTHER/FATHER: Well, I'm glad you haven't, because nothing you said or did caused your mother/father and I to divorce. You are not to blame in any way. And if you ever have any thoughts or feelings like that, I want you to come talk to me about them. Okay?

Or perhaps the child answered yes.

> MOTHER/FATHER: Oh, then how do you think you may have caused it?
>
> The child gives an explanation.
>
> MOTHER/FATHER: No, that is just not true. You had nothing to do with the reason for our divorce. And it certainly was not because [you were bad, did something wrong, we were mad at you, or whatever other explanation the child provided].

Still another way to respond is to give the child a clear explanation such as this:

> Mary, I want you to know that you are not responsible or to blame for our divorce in any way. It's not your fault. You didn't cause it. Remember when we talked about how some things are adult business and some things are children's business? Well, divorce is strictly adult business, it's not a child's decision to make. That means it is just between Mommy/Daddy and me, and not you.

I have already addressed the three primary concerns children have in response to the initial marital disruption. Parents should be alert for these fears and misconceptions in their children and should follow the guidelines suggested for helping children with them. Before going on to other divorce-related issues, I want to address some questions parents often have about discussing these issues with children.

Guidelines for Parent–Child Discussions

Children's separation anxieties, reunification fantasies, and their assumption of blame for the divorce are all deeply felt concerns that influence their ability to adjust to marital separation. These concerns can only be resolved through explanations and discussions between parent and child. However, a single statement or one sitting is not enough to fully reassure children about their permanent and continuing relationship or to convince a child that the divorce is final. The issues for children are too profound and emotionally charged to be resolved so easily. Parents must have frequent discussions with their children about all of these topics. Several guidelines for helping parents with these discussions follow.

What is the best way to approach children? Parents do not need to wait for the child to initiate a conversation. Instead, they should bring up the subjects identified here. As demonstrated in the sample scripts, parents can give children factual explanations and engage them in a dialogue that draws out the children's own understanding of the divorce. For example, parents might ask children to elaborate on their thoughts and feelings about each topic by saying, "Let's talk some more about the divorce. Tell me again what you think you did to cause the divorce." Once children have fully presented their perception of events, parents can much more effectively clear up their misconceptions.

Children almost always respond readily to candid questioning. If parents ask direct, matter-of-fact questions, children will give surprisingly honest and revealing answers. Almost all children will willingly share their thoughts and feelings if they are sure it is safe to talk to their parents about the divorce. If children cannot respond to repeated invitations from parents to talk about the divorce, then they do not feel safe in doing so. This hesitancy stems from two sources.

Parents must accept the fact that children who cannot talk about the divorce feel that it is risky for them to do so. Such reticent children have often learned that parents do not want to hear or cannot accept what they have to say. For example, parents may not be able to tolerate their children's sadness about the divorce or their anger at parents for leaving. In order to be emotionally connected to children and capable of providing genuine reassurances, parents must be able to accept children's negative reactions to the divorce. Parents must be tolerant of critical perceptions or hurt feelings that they, understandably, often do not want to hear.

The other reason why children are reluctant to talk with parents is because loyalty conflicts make disclosure unsafe. In these cases, children are covertly pressured to take sides in parental conflicts, or one parent uses what the child has said as ammunition to get back at the other parent. We examine the significant problems that result from these loyalty conflicts in chapter 8.

How do parents know whether their children believe their explanations or whether they are especially troubled by a particular topic? There are certain signals that parents can learn to recognize. For example, if some aspect of the divorce is too upsetting for children to talk about, they will often change the subject. To illustrate, Mrs. Brown may say to her five-year-old son, Johnny, "Let's talk some more about the fact that Daddy and I are going to get a divorce." If Johnny quickly replies, "Look at the pretty bird out on the swing," Mrs. Brown should be alerted to a problem her son is having with accepting the divorce. This type of response is called avoidance or denial. Most children will try to deny unwanted aspects of the divorce, and parents must sensitively but firmly refocus their attention on the reality at hand.

Mrs. Brown could say, "Johnny, I know that you do not like it when I tell you that Daddy and I are not going to be married any more. But I need you to know that we are going to divorce and that is not going to change. You and I should talk some more about what is going to happen when Daddy and I divorce. Tell me, what do you think is the worst thing that will happen when Daddy and I move apart?"

It is very possible that Johnny will continue to reject any discussion of the divorce. For example, Johnny's response to his mother's questions might be: "Be quiet! I don't want to talk about divorce. I want you and Daddy to stay married and live here with me." Mrs. Brown could then reply, "I know you wish we would stay married, but that is not going to happen. Let's talk some more about the divorce. I wonder if you're afraid sometimes that Mommy and Daddy won't love you as much or won't be with you as much after the divorce. We have talked about this before, but tell me again what you think is going to happen when Daddy moves out on Saturday?"

The staging of these parent–child discussions is also important. Children will spontaneously ask questions and make comments if they feel that their parents are comfortable about discussing the divorce. Parents can also encourage free expression by responding to children whenever they bring up divorce-related issues. Parents will find it is most effective to initiate discussions about the divorce during a normally quiet and close time. Bedtime is an especially good opportunity to talk together about the divorce. The mother or father could, for example, rub the child's back while they talk together about the child's concerns. Such a setting will help children express what may be worrying them. However, parents should not insist on disclosure when children really do not wish to talk. These topics are painful and children should have some control over when and how they manage them.

Responding to Sadness

In order to provide effective explanations for the divorce, parents must be prepared to respond to their children's inevitable sadness and help them deal with it. Although children certainly need explanations, parents must expect these discussions to evoke intense sadness in themselves and in their children. Let's examine this more closely.

The entire process of explaining the divorce to children will be sad. It is hard to give them clear expectations of what is going to happen, to invite them to ask questions about the divorce and give suggestions for how to make things better for them, and to address their concerns in the forthright ways suggested here. When providing explanations, parents should feel free to share their sadness and regrets about the divorce with their children. Parents and children alike need to grieve the loss of the family as they have known it, and seeing the parent's sadness gives children permission to mourn their own loss. Parents must also be realistic and acknowledge to themselves and to their children that the divorce is going to be hard for everyone. Children will be sad, afraid, and sometimes angry; and parents will also feel sad and often guilty.

In particular, however, it is children's sadness that many loving, responsible, and otherwise capable parents cannot tolerate or respond to effectively. Parents often want the child to stop feeling sad in order to manage their own painful feelings and so they pressure the child to deny these feelings.

Parents often respond ineffectively to their children's sadness, a problem that becomes increasingly significant over time because the child's sadness does not simply go away. For years after the divorce, children continue to have sad feelings at times about the loss of their original intact family. How parents respond to these feelings of sadness, loss, and vulnerability will be an important factor in determining how well children adjust to the divorce. Children adjust better when parents offer a supportive and understanding response to the child's sadness, rather than avoiding or denying these feelings or feeling inadequate and immobilized by them, as so often occurs.

Our Culture Denies Sad Feelings

The Russians say that Americans "have no soul," by which they mean that we are afraid of the sad and empty feelings that are an ordinary and natural part of everyday life. It seems that we want to turn away from these feelings and deny that they exist, without experiencing or acknowledging them. At least in terms of divorce, there is some truth to that Russian saying. Children are sad and often lonely during the divorce process, and they need support from grandparents, clergy, neighbors, teachers, and others. Most children do not get this emotional support, however. For example, one study reported that less than ten percent of children had an adult speak sympathetically to them as the divorce unfolded!

The problem is not that people don't care. Many kind adults see these children's distress and care deeply about them. However, they aren't sure whether it is better for the child to address these sad feelings or to politely ignore them. Adults are also afraid that if they address these feelings, they might say the wrong thing and make the child feel worse. However, the child will fare far better when parents and other adults can accept these difficult feelings and approach them directly, so that the child is not alone with them.

Adults can do this simply by acknowledging children's sad and hurt feelings and offering their genuine affection and concern.

The initial period of marital disruption is very sad for most children. Children see their parents fighting, hurting each other, and crying. Children also watch one parent move out of the home, and hear unwanted explanations that their parents are going to divorce. Almost all children will be profoundly sad during the first few months following the breakup. Unfortunately, parents are often unable to respond to their children's sadness because of their own feelings of loss, guilt over the divorce, or discomfort with sadness in general. As a result, children do not receive the comfort they need during this difficult period.

Ineffective responses to children's sadness about the breakup almost always spring from some form of denial. Parents usually do this by trying to ignore children's sadness or, if that is not possible, by invalidating their feelings by trying to talk children out of them. Let's look more closely at the most common types of ineffective responses.

First, parents can just ignore the child's sad feelings. In some cases, parents are so caught up in their own distress that they cannot refocus on their children's experience.

In other families, denial of feelings in general prevents parents from confronting their children's grief. In these families no one is ever allowed to feel sad. Every family has unspoken rules governing emotional expression—which feelings can be expressed, at what intensity, under what circumstances, and to whom. However, some families have an unspoken but clearly understood rule that no one in the family is ever sad, or that only certain family members are allowed to feel sadness, such as girls or the youngest child. Such a family rule is problematic, of course, but manageable until a family crisis such as divorce occurs. With divorce, feelings become stronger and the sadness cannot be denied or ignored without creating more serious problems by trying to maintain the family rule against sadness.

At other times, parents want their children to be unaffected by the divorce in order to confirm the decision to divorce. Here again, such parents place too much control over their own well-being in the child's hands. If the child is sad or weepy, the parent takes this as evidence that divorcing was the wrong course; if the child seems happy, the parent feels the decision to divorce was correct. These parents try to avert their children's legitimate sadness by trying to cheer them up, often by overstimulating children with too many activities in order to keep them busy and "happy." These parents accurately anticipate that if children are allowed quiet, unstructured time, tears will sometimes emerge.

Other parents may invalidate the child's experience more overtly, by statements like: "Stop feeling sorry for yourself like that. You don't really have anything to be sad about. Other kids have much bigger problems than you do. You should just be thankful for all the things you do have and knock those tears off." Children subjected to this kind of advice will comply with the parental demand and stop looking weepy, but the sadness will go underground and be masked. Sadness, a healthy and natural response to marital disruption, then gives way to chronic depression (boredom, listlessness, loss of interests, and lack of motivation) or to agitation, excessive activity, unfocused attention, constant sensation seeking, and careless risk taking.

An even greater mistake than denying the child's sad feelings is to actively denigrate them. Boys, in particular, are likely to be shamed for sadness and contemptuously judged as "weak." For example, it is more common than many think for parents to say, "Stop crying like a baby" or "Don't be such a big sissy." Young boys are just as sad about the breakup as girls, but their sadness is more often rejected. Researchers have found that lack of emotional support for sad feelings is one of the reasons why divorce is harder for boys than for girls.

When children's sadness, vulnerability, or longing for the intact family is denied in one of these ways, children cannot adjust well. These painful feelings cannot be resolved because they are not allowed to run their natural course. Children caught in one of the circumstances described previously will soon become afraid of their sadness and rather than feeling sad or weepy, they will become anxious and confused. As children lose touch with their sadness, they also lose touch with other emotions and other aspects of their experience. These children, in effect, lose touch with themselves. Furthermore, when children's legitimate feelings of sadness over the divorce are denied, they do not develop the capacity for empathy and compassion. And, as strange as this may sound initially, they do not develop the capacity to be alone that is essential to mature functioning. As a result, these children will often be more demanding of adult attention, require constant stimulation and entertainment, and feel more restless or agitated.

On the other hand, sometimes children do just feel sorry for themselves or use suffering to manipulate their guilty parents. In some situations, one parent may foster and encourage a child's sadness as a way to blame or get back at the other. In the majority of cases, however, children do not receive the comfort they need because parents feel inadequate and don't know how to respond to their sadness. However, parents can take several steps to help children successfully manage their sad and hurt feelings.

Responding Effectively to Children's Sadness

Although parents can respond effectively to their children's sadness in many different ways, these responses often will include the following three-step sequence.

First, parents must *acknowledge* the sad feelings and approach them directly, not deny or ignore them in the hope that they will pass away on their own. If done sincerely, it is remarkably effective to simply acknowledge the sadness by bending over to children's height, looking kindly into their eyes, putting your hand gently on their shoulder, and saying something like: "You seem a little bit sad right now."

Parents also need to accept children's feelings and *validate* them, not diminish them or try to talk children out of them. For example, parents can confirm the child's experience by saying: "Of course you have unhappy feelings about all of this. You don't want us to go apart, you want us to stay together. I know that the divorce is hard for you and understand that you feel sad about it sometimes."

Finally, parents need to *comfort* their children with affection and understanding, not try to "fix" the feelings or insist that children be happy when they are not. For example, parents can offer such comfort by saying: "Come, sit with me and let me hold you. What's the saddest thing about the divorce for you right now? Tell me about it so I can understand better."

If parents can directly approach their child's sadness with such comfort and understanding, the feelings will run their natural course and the child will soon move on to other, happier, moods. Responding to the sadness is also the most effective way to begin talking with children about their worries and concerns. For example, in response to being asked what they think is the saddest thing about the divorce, children often express fears of being left, of losing parents, of being responsible for the divorce, or other issues that parents can address and help resolve. The following case example illustrates these principles.

Five-year-old Gene was having the worst Christmas ever. His parents had split up just before Thanksgiving and his father had moved out of their house and into his own apartment. There had been a lot of arguing and confusion about whom he was going to spend Christmas with. Finally, they decided that he would spend Christmas eve with his mother and Christmas morning with his father. On Christmas night he was going to have dinner with his grandparents, Papa and Nana, with whom he had always been especially close.

When his father brought Gene to his grandparent's house on Christmas evening, he told them that Gene hadn't behaved very well and that Christmas hadn't been as much fun as it usually was. His father didn't like how "greedy" Gene had seemed as raced through opening his presents, without stopping to appreciate them or thank anybody for them. An old friend of the family who had stopped by to wish them a Merry Christmas jokingly said that watching Gene open his presents was like watching a "shark feeding frenzy." As soon as Gene finished opening all of his presents—which only took a few minutes even though there were many of them—he started whining, "What else do I get? What else do I get?" His father told Papa and Nana that it hadn't been a very good Christmas with Gene and that he didn't think things had gone much better with his mother the night before.

As soon as he came in the house, Nana knew that Gene was out of sorts and feeling blue. Nana tried to take him by the hand and show him their Christmas presents and decorations, but Gene shied away from her. Nana brought out some of Gene's favorite toys, special things that she kept at her house just because Gene loved to play with them, but they didn't hold his interest as they usually did.

Nana was patient but kept failing in her bids to engage him, and Gene seemed lost as he wandered half-heartedly from toy to toy and room to room.

After following Gene's aimless movements around the house for a while, Nana could see that he was not settling in and warming up as he usually did. Trying to acknowledge the sadness she saw in his face, Nana suggested, "Is our big boy a little bit sad today? Will you let me hold you in my lap for a minute?"

Gene brushed off her invitation, backed away, and stared down at the floor. Seeing that Gene was feeling miserable, Nana reassured him. "You're sad today, but you don't want me to hold you right now. That's okay. I'll stay here in my chair and just watch you play."

Gene remained distant and restless, and Nana stayed in her chair and watched as he became even more frustrated with whatever he tried to play with. Gene did not want to maintain his distance for long, however, and a few minutes later he came over to her chair and asked, "Can I sit with you?" Nana gathered Gene up into her lap, held him close, and rocked him quietly. Gene soon said, "I wish Mom and Dad would get married again." Nana appreciated that feeling and said, "Yes, of course you do. It's been sad today because your family wasn't together." Gene nodded, sank more deeply into his grandmother's lap, and they talked some more about the divorce. In just a few minutes, however, Gene's face brightened as he noticed a favorite toy in the room and asked Nana if they could play with it together. With this transition to a happier mood and shared interaction, Gene became interested in his play again and an especially close and loving evening ensued.

As this story shows, children may be especially vulnerable to their sadness around holidays and birthdays, and parents often feel uncomfortable with their sadness and pressure children to be happy. This is what happened to Gene at both his mother's and father's house and, in part, why he was so restless, irritable, unresponsive, and distracted.

As Nana did, parents need to let children be sad and miss things when they are feeling this way. In these moments, parents should be accepting and responsive to children, without trying to talk them out of their feelings or make them feel bad about being sad, missing the other parent, or longing for their old family to be together again. If the parent can be supportive and emotionally responsive to the child's unhappiness, the sadness will soon run its course and come to a natural close, freeing the child to spontaneously move on to other interests and activities. Many boys, in particular, channel their sadness into anger and depression in the aftermath of divorce. One of the best ways to prevent this consequence is for mothers and fathers to accept their children's sadness about the divorce and comfort them in their distress.

We turn now from children's concerns during the initial breakup to parental guidelines for the divorce.

PART THREE

Guidelines for Parents

5

Parental Conflict
and Cooperation

Research shows that in the years after a divorce, the most poorly adjusted children are those whose parents involve them in continuing conflicts. Children suffer when parents expose them to parental battles, when they criticize each other to the children, and when they fight through the children. When parental anger is expressed in these ways, children develop longstanding problems, including poor grades, frequent fights with friends, defiance, and disobedience. It is very damaging when one parent says, "Your mother is crazy. You don't have to do what she says" or "You don't have to pay attention to your father; he only sees you on weekends. I'm the one who is really raising you." Because children are exposed to parental hostilities so often, and because continuing parental conflicts are so problematic for children, we must examine them closely.

Without question, the single biggest problem for children of divorce is being exposed to continuing parental conflict. Parents commonly become enraged during the divorce process and routinely blame each other for everything that has gone wrong. Embittered parents who feel justified in their rage because the other parent has rejected, betrayed, or abandoned them often cannot see their own contribution to the problems of the marriage. Women and men who are able to grow through the experience of divorce and go on to fulfill their hopes for a better life must be able to step beyond the victim stance and stop unloading exclusive responsibility for the breakup onto the former spouse. If not, this anger and blame fuels the chronic parental conflict that is so problematic for children.

Parents must realize how much children suffer when they are embroiled in parental battles and take steps to manage their anger responsibly, shield children from parental conflicts, and work cooperatively in the child's best interest.

Protecting Children from Parental Hostilities

Chronic Parental Conflict Hurts Children

All parents will have disagreements and become angry with each other at times. If these conflicts are not threatening and pervasive, they are a normal part of human relationships and are not destructive for children. However, in many divorcing families, parental conflict is so intense and unrelenting that it has very negative effects on children.

Divorce is widely believed to hurt children and cause long-term adjustment problems. And researchers have found that, on average, children of divorce exhibit more problems and have a lower level of well-being than children from intact families. But research has also shown that the divorce as such and the structural changes in the family do not cause these adjustment problems—they result from increased exposure to parental conflict. We must examine this critical distinction closely.

Researchers have found that about a third of the children who have experienced parental divorce are very well-adjusted. Why do these children cope so well? The most important reason is that these healthy children have parents who cooperate or do not expose children to parental conflicts. Conversely, researchers have found that the most poorly adjusted children have relentlessly embattled and litigious parents. In almost every case, children with long-term adjustment problems have been exposed to continued parental conflict. Thus, the effects of chronic marital conflict must be considered separately from the more general effects of divorce. All parents must learn that chronic marital conflict is the culprit that causes serious and longlasting problems for children.

Furthermore, chronic marital conflict is not just damaging to children in divorced families, it is just as harmful to children in intact families. In general, the degree of marital discord is one of the most important determinants of children's adjustment in all families. Thus, children in intact families with high marital conflict have more adjustment problems than children from low-conflict intact families. As in divorced families, research has found that children from high-conflict, intact families have more aggressive and defiant behavior problems, more emotional symptoms of anxiety and depression, and lower self-esteem than those in low-conflict, intact homes. Thus, the message to divorcing parents is clear: they must not fight in front of children or embroil them in their conflicts.

Sadly, however, this message often goes unheeded. Angry attempts to punish former spouses and disrupt their relationship with their children are commonplace. And many children are exposed to intense scenes of parental conflict both before and after the divorce. Parental acrimony usually peaks at the time of marital separation, and during this period most children witness bitter and explosive interactions between their parents. One grim study reported that one-fourth of children in middle and upper-middle class homes had witnessed physical violence between their parents at the time of marital separation. Let's look more closely at the reasons why marital conflict is so harmful to children.

Parental cooperation, or at least the absence of overt conflict, is essential for children's secure adjustment. Parents must acknowledge that children will not adjust successfully as long as intense parental hostilities continue. Why are children so affected by hatred between their parents? Children are frightened when they see their parents shout at, berate, and threaten each other. Although some older children may try to distance themselves and affect aloof disinterest, they are terrified that harm will befall both their parents and themselves. Children are intensely concerned about the safety and well-being of their all-important attachment figures and rightly know that they are not secure as long as their parents are threatened. Because they are focused on the former spouse, however, combative parents cannot see the worry in their children's faces or recognize the intense anxiety that creates the sleep disturbances and hypervigilance that their children usually suffer from.

Whenever I am talking with children of embattled parents I ask them, "If I had a magic wand and could grant you any three wishes you wanted, what would you most like to have?" Without exception, their first wish is always, "I wish my parents would stop fighting." Many children go on to ask the same things with their second and third wishes as well. In other words, children cannot imagine wanting anything other than to have their parents stop fighting. Children are frightened when their parents fight and, poignantly, often secretly pray that they will stop.

Children's intense worries about their parents and anxiety about their own safety and well-being are exacerbated by problems that arise as interparental conflict stresses parents and reduces their ability to comfort and parent their children. And, as if insecurity and loss of effective parenting were not enough, these children also feel *responsible* for parental hostilities. As detailed in chapters 3 and 4, children believe they are responsible for all of the major occurrences in their lives—including parental fighting. This egocentric tendency is exacerbated by the issues that parents often fight about. That is, children routinely listen to their parents fight over them. As a result, there is little doubt in children's minds that they are to blame for this unhappiness, even though they do not want it and feel helpless to stop it.

Finally, although chronic marital conflict is destructive for all children, it seems to be especially harmful to boys. Researchers have found that, on average, boys are more vulnerable to the adverse effects of family conflict and cannot cope with it as effectively as girls. One reason is that in most families girls are more protected from family conflict than boys, both before the divorce and afterwards. Researchers have found that parents fight more and that their fights continue longer in the presence of sons than daughters.

Parental Conflicts Can Be Managed Responsibly

Although parents expect divorce to end their marital problems, they are often dismayed to find that conflict continues in the period following the initial breakup. In particular, participation in the legal system often intensifies problems over custody and visitation. As detailed in chapter 7, if family law attorneys are adversarial and attempt to win custody, the anger and distrust between former spouses are especially likely to be exacerbated and often endure unabated for years after the final court decree. This result is a grave problem for children who consequently experience far more stress, unhappiness, and insecurity in homes with interparental hostility.

A parent who fights with the former spouse in front of their children must stop this destructive interaction, even if the other parent continues to do so. Parents who are unable to shield children from such warfare must seek professional help. There are three basic steps toward establishing a more cooperative parenting relationship after divorce.

STEP ONE: INTERNAL RESOLVE. The first step toward managing anger and conflict responsibly is to acknowledge that children are harmed by chronic parental conflict and to make a personal commitment to shield children from it. Every divorcing parent should contemplate this fact and try to hold to this resolve as much as possible. Remember, it is intense continued hostilities between parents, not isolated conflicts that inevitably occur, that harms children.

This internal commitment to protect children from parental conflict should be made personally and privately, regardless of what the other parent does. Even if one parent continues to behave irresponsibly, this does not give the other parent permission to respond in kind. The concept of an island of psychological safety can help parents achieve this goal.

If both parents join the parental battle, children lose emotional access to both of them. There is no safe shelter from the storm. But if one parent can exercise restraint and not retaliate destructively, children lose psychological access to the other parent but still have emotional contact with the restrained parent. With the support of one parent, these children are sad, but not depressed about the parental conflict. Unlike children with two warring parents, these children do not fail in school or act out angrily and defiantly. Although these children are exposed to parental pain and conflict, they also have the support necessary to cope because they have one parent who does not undermine the other or pressure them to take sides. Having emotional contact with this neutral parent allows children to tolerate family turmoil without developing symptoms or maladaptive defenses. Thus, as long as one parent refrains from joining the battle, children retain a much-needed island of psychological safety that is lost when both parents become embattled.

Even though children adjust far better when one parent exercises restraint, this unwillingness to retaliate when provoked is clearly the hard part of step one. However, it does take two to tango, and if one parent makes a sincere effort to shield children from parental conflicts, family life will improve immediately and significantly for children. Don't take my word for it, try it for yourself and see. Ideally, of course, it is best if both parents can discuss the harmful impact of parental conflicts and can mutually agree to terminate angry conversations until the children are not present.

STEP TWO: HAND SIGNALS TO TERMINATE ESCALATING CONFLICT. Angry former spouses must find ways to manage conflicts between them so that arguments do not escalate out of control. Despite the best of intentions, tempers flare when certain topics are addressed. At these moments conflicts escalate out of control and children are exposed to hitting and yelling, insults and threats, tears and pain. Divorcing couples must have a mechanism to decisively terminate such interactions as soon as they begin, and hand signals are a disarmingly simple but effective method.

On behalf of their children, divorcing couples should mutually agree to abide by the following system. Whenever one parent feels that a discussion with the other is hurtful, unproductive, or about to escalate emotionally, the parent should raise an index finger in the air to signal "be still." As soon as either parent gives this signal the conversation stops immediately. No one gets in the last word. No one challenges or criticizes why the signal was given (for example, "You always use that signal just to . . ."). Both parties simply stop talking about that topic for five minutes, without further discussion and without exceptions. By giving and following the signal, appropriate controls over escalating emotions have been instituted. After five minutes, parents can mutually decide whether they wish to continue talking about the previous topic, try talking about something else, or whether to terminate their conversation for today and go their separate ways.

If both parties agree to use this method, each parent gains needed control over the delicate communication process. Each parent possesses a stop button that provides a safe way out of escalating conflicts. Both parents are reassured to know that they have a time-out in which to regroup and gain some emotional distance. When parents feel out of control in the relationship, they are most likely to interact in ways that are destructive for children to witness. In contrast, when adults can effectively control their own emotions and relationships, children immediately feel more safe and secure. Parents will observe a direct correlation between their ability to exercise control over conflicts in their relationship and children's sense of safety and security.

STEP THREE: GUIDELINES FOR EFFECTIVE COMMUNICATION. Many men and women have relatively limited communication skills and almost everyone is uncomfortable when negotiating emotionally charged conflicts in close personal relationships. Divorcing couples are confronted with an extraordinarily challenging task. They must be able to communicate and resolve conflicts over the most important things in their lives—their children—with someone they may distrust, fear, or hate. Nevertheless, parents need to cooperate and communicate with each other about many child-related concerns. Who will pick up the children from school? When will they go to summer camp? How will they handle notes from teachers about meetings and conferences at school? Who will be taking them shopping for new school clothes? Divorced parents are continually presented with the need to make joint decisions about their child's daily activities and to discuss the values by which they want to raise their child. There are no easy answers to such a profound task, but helpful guidelines are available to structure the difficult negotiations that divorcing couples face. The following list presents ten of the most basic guidelines for effective communication.

1. Establish a hand signal to terminate conversations that could deteriorate into conflicts. Do not continue arguing when the other person gives the signal to stop the conversation for five minutes.
2. Stick to the problem at hand and deal with only one issue at a time. Do not bring up past problems or expand the current conflict to other topics.
3. Keep the conflict contained within the parental dyad. Do not drag in references to friends or relatives who agree with you. For example, refrain from saying, "Even your mother says . . ."
4. Treat your former spouse respectfully and refrain from

provocations. Do not yell, insult, use obscene language, or resort to name-calling. Offending the other person will only escalate problems.

5. Stay physically and emotionally engaged with the discussion at hand until it is finished. Do not withdraw or walk out of the room to avoid conflict without warning your former spouse first. Walking out is often a manipulative ploy. If you choose to exit, first give the other person one chance to change. For example, "I am invoking the hand signal right now and you are not responding. If you do not stop talking about this immediately, I am leaving" or "I don't like the way you are treating me right now. Stop it immediately or I am going to leave."

6. Agree on mutually satisfactory times to talk. Do not negotiate under the influence of drugs or alcohol.

7. Focus only on the problems that need to be resolved. Do not try to physically intimidate your former spouse or play on his or her insecurities.

8. Listen attentively to the other person's point of view. Do not pretend to listen while actually shutting them out and formulating your own rebuttal.

9. Communicate about specific behaviors without using pejorative labels. For example, "You were twenty minutes late to pick her up today" is far more effective than saying "You're always late to pick her up; you're too selfish to care about anyone else's needs." Do not use generalizations such as "you always" or "you never."

10. Accept responsibility for your share of what went wrong. Do not assign blame, rigidly resist your former spouse's viewpoint, or insist that your perception of events is the only version of the truth.

By employing these ten rules, divorcing couples will avoid the most common pitfalls of conflict negotiation. Of course, the success of these guidelines depends on both parties agreeing to abide by them as much as possible (no one can be expected to do it right all of the time). A neutral mediator will be necessary if one party is unwilling to cooperate, if one party feels physically threatened, or if emotions are too volatile. A professional divorce mediator is usually available through the Family Law Division at your local county courthouse.

Expressing Parental Conflicts Through the Children

One of the strongest determinants of how well a child adjusts to divorce is whether the former spouses support each other in their continuing relationship as parents. Although this cooperation is essential for the child's secure adjustment, it is often difficult for parents to achieve. When two people divorce there is usually a great deal of hurt, anger, and distrust between them. Both must cope with difficult feelings of betrayal, rejection, and failure. As a result, former spouses may continue to vent their anger and bitterness toward each other for many years after the divorce. Unfortunately, however, one of the most common ways that parental hostilities are expressed is through the children. In particular, these hostilities are often acted out irresponsibly by undermining the former spouse's relationship with the children or by disparaging the former spouse to the children. Without exception, children develop enduring psychological problems when a parent communicates anger toward the former spouse in ways that erode the other's parenting authority.

Before examining the consequences when one spouse undermines another, let's consider what I am suggesting by a cooperative or supportive parental relationship after divorce. What can this realistically mean? Do parents still need to love each other, be friends, or even like each other? No. Furthermore, there is no need for parents to pretend to their children that they have positive feelings for the former spouse. However, parents do need to support one another in their relationship with the children. In other words, each spouse must communicate to the children that the other is still their parent, cares for them deeply, and should be respected and obeyed. This step is very difficult for some parents to take because they are so angry at their former spouse; however, it is in the children's best interest to have a positive relationship with both parents, rather than having one parent devalued as a role model.

Children Suffer When Parents Undermine Each Other

It is destructive when one parent undermines another with comments such as: "Your mother doesn't know what she's doing. Come to me if she tries to tell you what to do" or "Your father's a jerk. Why do you want to see him?"

Why are these criticisms so difficult for children to deal with? There are many reasons, but one of the most important ones is that children identify with their parents. When parents disparage each other, it is almost the same as criticizing the child. Children are so closely identified with their parents that it is difficult for them to separate their mother's rejection of their father from their mother's rejection of them. In a psychological sense, children feel as if they are the same as their parents.

Although parents only intend to disparage the other parent, children react to these criticisms as if they were directed against them. This identification will be especially strong between a child and the same-sexed parent. For instance, it is almost impossible for a daughter to grow up and feel good about herself as a woman if her father continually disparaged her mother as being "fat" or "stupid." Boys who hear their mother subtly criticize their father will suffer similar consequences. With this identification between parent and child in mind, consider a typical family scenario in which Bob is undermining Carrie's parenting authority to the children.

Carrie and Bob had been divorced for eighteen months. The two children lived with Carrie during the week and with Bob and his new wife on weekends. Things had not gone well for Carrie since the divorce. Being a single parent was harder than she had imagined and she felt pulled in too many directions at once. She was working part-time, taking a few classes toward a college degree, and trying to carry on a relationship with a man she enjoyed dating.

All of these demands would have been manageable if not for her two children, who simply would not cooperate with her on anything. They were impossible for her to deal with. In fact, Carrie often thought that her children had joined in a conspiracy to ruin her life. For example, seven-year-old Bobby would mercilessly taunt Carrie's boyfriend whenever he came over. Although she threatened and spanked Bobby and sent him to his room, he succeeded in making the couple's evenings together miserable. Eventually, Carrie's boyfriend did not want to visit her at the house anymore, so she had to pay for a babysitter whenever they got together. Carrie was furious at her son and felt helpless. It seemed as if her son were trying to drive away the only source of emotional support and pleasure in her life.

Things were equally bad with her thirteen-year-old daughter, Sara. Sara regularly called her mother "fat," "stupid," and "ugly," as her brother did. It was as if her daughter had an uncanny ability to sense what insult would get under Carrie's skin and really hurt her. As with Bobby, Carrie could not control her daughter's obnoxious behavior. Carrie's efforts to talk with her daughter and try to understand her were no more successful than her threats, restrictions, and punishments. After many months of failure, Carrie hardly even tried to change her children. She felt that they hated her and she became increasingly depressed.

Her good friend and neighbor, Jean, first helped Carrie realize what was going on. Jean had observed that Bobby and Sara treated their mother worst right after they returned from a weekend with their father. Jean had also overheard a telephone conversation with their father in which the children had laughed at and made fun of Carrie. Jean knew that Carrie and Bob had not gotten along well after the divorce, but she hadn't realized that Bob had been encouraging the children's obnoxious behavior. Their laughter on the phone made it clear that Bob was thoroughly enjoying the problems that the children were creating for Carrie.

"All right, so now I know. But what can I do about it?" Carrie asked when Jean told her what she thought was going on. "He hates me, and now he has the kids hating me, too. I can't make him stop, he'll just laugh at me. All three of them will probably get together and just laugh at me."

In this all-too-common scenario, Carrie's life is painfully out of control because Bob has undermined her relationship with her children. And although it may not be obvious yet, Carrie's children are hurting as well. They are beginning a lifelong journey down a road of problems with self-esteem and intimacy. Let's first look at what is happening to the children and then see what Carrie can do to resolve her problem.

In this example, Bobby and Sara see their mother as someone they can abuse and control. Their father is teaching them that it is acceptable to provoke and defy their mother. When children are allowed to treat a parent in this defiant, disrespectful way, their attitude will extend to other adults in their lives as well. Bobby and Sara will probably come to regard teachers, principals, camp counselors, and coaches with similar disdain. These children are learning that they do not have to treat others with respect or comply with rules and regulations, an antisocial message that is very serious because it often leads children to behave in illegal, exploitative, or physically abusive ways when they are older. This antisocial tendency is exacerbated by their parents' role model, which shows that anger and contempt are acceptable ways to relate to others. The children's ability to form caring and mutually respectful relationships will be impaired throughout their lives if this pattern is not rectified.

Sara and Bobby also lose a role model when their mother is perceived as someone to be discounted. As her daughter, Sara will have to reject her "weak" and powerless mother and try not to become like her. In doing so, she will lose her most important role model for learning what it means to be a woman. At the same time that Sara tries to push her mother away, she is also likely to adopt the same negative characteristics she has attributed to her mother and grow up feeling that she too is "fat, stupid, and ugly." Typically, she will select a marriage partner who treats her in the same disparaging manner.

In parallel, Bobby will learn that women and wives do not deserve affection or respect. He will have great difficulty in developing an egalitarian love relationship with a woman as he matures. In identifying with his father, he is likely to generalize this contemptuous attitude to other women and regard them callously as well.

Parents are our most important teachers about relationships. All of us have gained important expectations about relationships from watching our parents' daily interactions for many years. From our parents' model we develop general "schemas" for what goes on between two people in close enduring relationships and learn expectations for what people can and cannot do together. How close can we be together? Which needs can be met and which must go unacknowledged? Can we often trust and depend on someone else? Sometimes? Never? Can we be close to more than one person at the same time, or do we always have to take sides and choose between relationships? Can people have differences but still remain together, or do conflicts inevitably force people apart? Can people resolve problems and find mutually satisfying solutions, or do people have to remain locked in pain and anger forever?

We learn answers to these and many other questions while growing up in our families. Although we may relearn or alter these schemas as we develop further relationships, these first models are the most important determinants of the satisfaction we will find in later relationships. If a parent expresses anger at the former spouse by undermining the parenting authority of the other, then children such as Bobby and Sara will have very poor road maps to guide them through life.

When Only One Parent Cooperates

Difficult problems arise when one parent sincerely tries to cooperate but the other parent does not. There are no easy answers to this exasperating situation, but useful guidelines are available that may help. Let's continue with the previous illustration.

Because Carrie's husband, Bob, encouraged their children to disobey and show disrespect for her, both Carrie and her children were suffering from his destructive and antagonistic behavior. Carrie felt helpless to change the situation. "I can't stop Bob from ruining my relationship with my children. He doesn't care how I feel. If I told him to stop, he'd ignore me or just laugh. He's never listened to me before or done what I've asked."

Carrie, and many others in similar situations, feel helpless. This sense of futility is often how they felt while they were married, when they did not think they were respected, listened to, or supported by their spouse. It is terribly frustrating to leave a marriage because of this kind of treatment, only to find that you have to live with the same problems after the divorce. In most cases, however, you do not have to endure the same problems. Carrie can use this situation as an opportunity to grow out of the old submissive role she had with her husband and learn to respond to him more assertively and directly.

How can she do this? Initially Carrie wanted her boyfriend to talk to Bob for her, but this approach would only have exacerbated feelings of competition and jealousy. The spouse who is undermined must speak directly to the former spouse about the problem; confronting the issue face-to-face provides the only real possibility of change. Although therapists, lovers, grandparents, and friends may be concerned, they cannot effectively intervene for the parent. The undermined parent must do this personally. The parent whose authority and standing have been eroded should contact the former spouse and request a meeting to talk about difficulties in their parental relationship. At the meeting, these parents should tell their former spouses what they do not like and what they want changed. The parents can communicate how they feel about being undermined and why the problem is making things difficult for the children. The former spouses should then be invited to respond, because they often have legitimate concerns that can be addressed. However, the parents should not enter into an argument about who is right or wrong. Rather, undermined parents should simply state again what kind of conduct they desire.

In addition, undermined parents must also reassure their former spouses that they will not undermine the former spouse's relationship with the children. For example, a parent might say, "I will not reciprocate by undermining your relationship with the children. I will support you in your role as a parent, and I want you to support me in mine." Often, after being directly confronted and assured that no reciprocal devaluation is going on, many spouses will reduce their criticism and manipulation.

If this first confrontation does not alleviate the problem, the undermined parent should then meet with the children and the former spouse together. In front of all concerned, the parent can repeat the request for the former spouse to stop undermining his or her relationship with the children. The parent can then ask the children to stop participating in this scheme, even if the former spouse continues to provoke them. Making the problem overt in this way usually diminishes the destructive alliance between the goading parent and the children. Again, the parent should assure the children and the former spouse that there will be no reciprocal undermining of their relationship. If a parent feels physically threatened by the former spouse, a third party can be quietly present (for example, a grandparent or mutual friend—not a new lover).

Carrie was able to stop this destructive pattern. She had the courage to confront Bob and her children with the problem. This action, coupled with setting firmer limits on the children's obnoxious behavior and presenting them with the option of living with their father if they preferred, largely resolved the situation. Carrie took control of her life and stopped allowing her former husband to victimize her. Only when she claimed equal power in the relationship did her husband and children become more respectful of her. Carrie had to assert her equality for herself, however—no one else could do it for her.

Ending the Marriage

Parents who cannot stop fighting with each other cannot end their marriage. Although it is a hateful connection, combative parents keep themselves linked together by remaining emotionally embroiled with each other. For litigious parents, in particular, the former spouse remains the emotional center of their universe as their inner worlds are organized around the unjust and hurtful things the other has done. Before they can end their battle and establish a more cooperative parental relationship, they must psychologically or internally end the marriage. This is hard work for everyone and is especially difficult for combative parents. Psychologically ending the marriage is harder than it sounds because a great deal more work is involved in this kind of separation than in just going through the legal process of divorce.

Two people may remain emotionally tied together—in effect, still married—years after the divorce decree. Getting a lawyer, moving out, and signing papers make up the external components of divorce. Someone can go through this procedure and still not really be divorced, just as one can go through a marriage ceremony without becoming married in the sense of being emotionally committed. Too little attention is given to the fact that the real business of divorcing is internal.

There are several aspects to internally ending the marriage. First, one must grieve or mourn. An inevitable sadness needs to be felt before the marriage can be left behind. Some parents must grieve for the person who has gone; all parents must grieve for their unfulfilled hopes and dreams for the relationship. Parents need to find their tears about this loss, but too often parents want to avoid their sadness. If so, they are much more likely to be consumed by their anger at the former spouse and, unwittingly, use their children as weapons in the ensuing battle.

Both partners must also accept that they will feel some ambivalence about ending the marriage. Good things are being left behind in the marriage as well as bad. Some spouses will try to avoid acknowledging these positive aspects of the relationship in order to lessen the guilt over leaving or to reduce the pain of being left. Even deeply embittered couples have shared joyful and pleasurable moments together, as well as the experience of creating a new life. Coming to terms with the reality of the divorce requires parents to acknowledge and accept their contradictory feelings.

In order to truly end a marriage, parents also need to see their own contribution to the problems of the relationship. There are few exceptions to the old adage that it takes two people to have an argument. When parents begin to see that they share responsibility for the marriage and stop putting all the blame for its dissolution on the former spouse, then they can truly end the marriage. Although well-meaning friends will often express their support for one partner by criticizing the other, such comments are not helpful for either spouse because they heap all the responsibility onto one and make it more difficult for the other to see how he or she contributed to the problems of the relationship.

Parents cannot psychologically end the marriage quickly, however. The whole process may take several years, especially if it has been a long marriage. If parents can begin the internal work of ending the marriage, however, it will help them gain the emotional distance necessary to establish a cooperative parental relationship after the divorce.

6

Children Need Their Mothers and Fathers

The shared act of conception entitles children to both a mother and a father. Tragically, however, the natural birthright to two parents is lost for most children in the aftermath of divorce. In nine out of ten cases of divorce, mothers receive primary physical custody of the children and "visitation" for fathers only every other weekend still occurs. For most noncustodial fathers, divorce not only ends their marriage but also their participation as a parent. One national survey found that forty-nine percent of children had not seen their father even once in the preceding twelve months, and fewer than one child in six saw their fathers once a week.

Fathers tend to see more of their children in the first two years after the breakup, but, as years go by, fathers generally see less of their children, especially as they remarry and have new children. Because of the belief that women, not men, should take care of children, many people are not concerned by fathers' unavailability. However, researchers have shown that one of the best determinants of a child's adjustment to divorce is the extent of the father's continuing involvement. This chapter examines the adverse consequences for children when fathers are not available and suggests how to help children have a continuing relationship with both of their parents.

Children Often Lose Both Parents Through Divorce

Chapter 2 explained that the single biggest problem for young children of divorce is the threat of losing their parents. This fear of being left is often realized to some extent. The personal crisis brought on by the breakup and the tremendous demands of being a single parent often make mothers far less available to their children. This stress and overload for mothers, coupled with many fathers' minimal involvement after the divorce, often diminish children's closeness to both parents. Thus, from the children's point of view, it often seems that they have lost both of their parents because of the divorce. This deeply felt sense of loss causes many of the symptoms and problems that children develop in response to marital separation.

Single Mothers Are Overwhelmed

In the first year or so following the marital separation, mothers are often preoccupied with their personal and financial concerns. As a result, they often become less available to their children and less effective as parents. Most mothers are profoundly upset by the breakup, even if they initiated it, and their efforts to cope with their feelings can distract them from their children's needs. In addition, mothers usually struggle with all the new demands of becoming a single parent—dating, establishing a new emotional support network, and, in many cases, finding a job and entering the work force. If the father is not actively involved, she must also take over some of his parenting functions, such as disciplining sons. This task is especially difficult for many single mothers because sons in both intact and divorced families are usually more disobedient toward mothers than fathers.

Thus, mothers without a parenting partner suffer from role overload. They have to do it all: go to work, clean the gutters and mow the yard, take care of the children every day, find time to take them to school or to the doctor, and do everything else. Unfortunately, at the same time the mother must adjust to this demanding role, children have heightened needs for consistency, effective discipline, and emotional responsiveness from parents. Despite their efforts that may be heroic, however, preoccupied and fatigued mothers simply do not have the time or energy to meet these heightened needs.

Furthermore, divorce precipitates a significant decline in the standard of living for most parents, especially in mother-headed families where the father does not assume an active parenting role. Some estimates suggest that twenty-five percent of fathers fail to make support payments and another quarter make them inconsistently. As a result, these single-mother families are often pushed below the poverty line, and this economic hardship increases the risk of problems for children. Children's nutrition and health suffer when they grow up in poverty, and private lessons, educational toys, books, home computers, and other factors in academic success are simply unavailable. In many cases, single mothers must move to low-income neighborhoods with poorly financed schools and recreational facilities. Children raised in such environments are likely to be exposed to crime, violence, and the stigmatization of poverty. Finally, these demanding role changes and economic hardships are made even more difficult because they occur all at once.

The cumulative result of all these stresses is that children receive less adult attention and less effective parenting than they did before the divorce. More specifically, researchers have found that divorced mothers do not have as much time for their children, do not eat dinner with them as often, do not put them to bed at such regular hours, and do not get them ready for school on time as often as they did before the divorce. Divorced mothers also monitor their children less closely than mothers in two-parent families. They know less about where their children are, who they are with, and what they are doing. Children of divorce are receiving less adult supervision than children from two-parent families and are more likely to be home alone or to spend time with their peers. These problems are exacerbated because the quality of care that parents provide also declines as divorced parents communicate less effectively with their children, are more erratic in enforcing discipline, are less affectionate with children, and provide them more chaotic, disorganized households.

Even the most capable and resilient mother finds it harder to meet the increased needs of her children during the divorce transition. And this negative cycle is made worse because the problems that accompany these growing demands on mothers are greatly increased by the diminishing availability of most fathers after divorce.

Divorced Fathers Are Not Active Parents

Whereas the emotional unavailability of mothers usually ends after a period of adjustment, divorce all too often means a permanent reduction in the extent and quality of father–child relationships. By the second year after the separation, mothers have generally regained their self-esteem and confidence. They have regained their previous level of competence as parents and their emotional availability to their children has improved. Unfortunately, this is not the case with fathers. In most cases, three years after the divorce there is little or no father–child interaction. This finding is troubling because the extent of their fathers' involvement is closely linked to children's adjustment.

Divorced fathers have a continuing personal and financial responsibility to their children, but they often fail to fulfill these obligations. Often fathers are blamed exclusively for being too selfish and uncaring to follow through on their child-rearing obligations. At times this accusation is true, and it is distressing when fathers turn away from parenting. But there is more to understanding this complex social problem than one-sidedly blaming men. Divorced fathers who do want to take an active parenting role face formidable obstacles. There are two primary reasons why so many fathers are uninvolved parents.

COMPETING POWER BASES AND ANGER BETWEEN PARENTS. As we will see in the next chapter, the traditional mothering role was institutionalized in the early 1900s by the Industrial Revolution. The transition from an agrarian to an urban society created distinct sex roles that established mutually exclusive and competing power bases in the family. While fathers were given much more power in the working world, mothers were given an equal but more covert power base in the realm of child-rearing. As a result of this rigid sex-role demarcation, many men and women still believe that children belong more to their mothers than to their fathers and that mothers are the real parent. Although this gender bias has been changing in the courts, it is still reflected in some states by the longstanding custom of awarding primary physical and legal custody to mothers and giving alternate weekend "visitation" to fathers.

As a result of these cultural influences, many fathers do not feel they have an important contribution to make to their child's development. Unfortunately, many mothers share this belief. National surveys reveal that the majority of mothers do not want their husbands to be more involved in child-rearing, and researchers have found that many divorced mothers were prepared to forego child support if they no longer had to be inconvenienced by visits from their former partner. Although this preconception is beginning to change, child-rearing is still considered a female activity. Mother is viewed as the expert in the realm of child-rearing, and father is relegated to a concerned assistant, at best. Although women's roles have expanded to include professional achievement and independence, there needs to be a reciprocal growth in men's roles to include nurturing and caring for children.

Continuing parental conflict also contributes to fathers' lack of involvement with their children. As detailed in chapter 5, the mutual bitterness and distrust often aroused by marital disruption does not end with the divorce decree. In Euripides' version of the classic Greek myth of Medea, Jason leaves Medea for a beautiful young princess. Contemplating the ultimate revenge, Medea swears, "He shall never see alive again the sons he had from me . . . this is the way to deal Jason the deepest wounds." In line with traditional sex roles, one means for mothers to vent their anger may be to align the children with her against their father. Researchers have consistently found that from one-third to one-half of all custodial mothers report that they interfere with or resist visitations as a means of expressing anger. In parallel, of course, fathers' primary means of retaliation is often withholding financial support.

Both mothers and fathers may embroil their children in parental battles by pressuring them to take sides. As discussed in chapter 8, these parents create loyalty conflicts for their children, either by being overtly angry and disparaging or subtly sad and hurt when children wish to be close to the other parent. Unfortunately, few children of divorce have permission from both parents to be equally involved with the other parent. However, because mothers are usually the primary caretakers before the divorce and, as a rule, children live with their mothers afterwards, children tend to be closer to their mothers than to their fathers. When pressured to choose between their parents, most children's emotional allegiance initially goes to their mothers. In these circumstances, the father's continuing involvement may, in effect, require his former wife's permission. Feeling powerless and controlled in this situation, some fathers simply depart and abandon parenting altogether.

Too often divorced fathers' absence from parenting is discounted. Although, fortunately, there is increasing pressure to force fathers to comply with child support payments, there is little corresponding interest in involving fathers personally with their children. Fathers need to be encouraged to continue their child-rearing role after the divorce, however. Children consistently tell researchers that they want more contact with their fathers and they suffer socially, emotionally, and intellectually when their fathers are uninvolved. Children often internalize responsibility for his departure and suffer a precipitous loss of self-esteem and initiative that is reflected in depression, poor school performance, failure in peer relationships, and sexual promiscuity.

Not only are children deprived when their fathers exit, but mothers and fathers suffer as well. When fathers commit to their children, their values are clarified and their lives hold more purpose and meaning. When fathers give up their children, they are giving up important parts of themselves as well. The greatest opportunity that life presents for men to express the nurturing and intuitive parts of themselves is lost, as well as the opportunity to come to terms with both the painful and the rewarding aspects of their own childhoods. At the same time, without the relief offered by a parental partner, mothers' lives are overtaxed by the demands placed on a single parent. Clearly, mother, father, and child all lose when the father is not an active parent after divorce. However, additional obstacles keep fathers from remaining fully involved.

TRADITIONAL MALE ROLES DO NOT PREPARE MEN FOR PARENTING. The traditional male sex role also constrains men's involvement with children because it does not encompass nurturing and caring behavior. For example, most people do not think of emotional responsiveness to children as masculine behavior. Touching, holding, sustained eye-to-eye contact, preparing lunch, tucking a child into bed, making up a story, and answering a thousand questions are not traditionally considered to be masculine behavior. This unfortunate socialization limits men's involvement with their children in nuclear families and in custodial arrangements that follow divorce.

This male socialization begins early in life. While growing up, boys in our culture are not encouraged to take care of children. I recall seeing a four-year-old playing "Daddy" and taking his doll for a walk in the stroller around my neighborhood. I went up to him and asked how his baby was doing today, and he said "fine." But then he asked if I thought it was okay for him to play this game. His friends and his teacher at preschool had all told him that playing with a doll was "girl stuff" and that boys didn't do it. So, he asked, did I think it was all right for him to take his baby for a walk?

The sex role stereotypes that we learn as children will guide our behavior as parents when we are adults. By and large, fathers and mothers have been brought up to believe that child-rearing is the mother's domain and that the father's contribution is primarily limited to financial support and discipline. As a result, in most families the daily activities of child care are still carried out by the mother. One direct outcome of this faulty socialization is that many fathers do not formulate any concrete plans for maintaining regular participation in child-rearing at the time of marital separation.

When I meet with divorcing parents, I ask the fathers, "What plans have you made to have continuing contact with your children?" Some fathers respond, "I haven't really made any plans for being with the kids. My wife has mostly taken care of them over the years and I assume that will continue after the divorce as well. That has always been her arena. I haven't had a very big role in raising my children."

Because they have defined mother as the real parent throughout their marriage, many fathers are not prepared to take on active parenting after divorce. Many fathers disengage because they don't know how to relate to their children effectively. Often their own fathers did not talk to them or spend much time with them as they were growing up, and as adults, these fathers still do not have effective role models because their friends or coworkers are rarely significantly involved in parenting. Without effective role models or social supports for adopting a significant parenting role, many fathers will not know how to relate to their children, let alone how to meet the complex and challenging tasks of taking care of them on a daily basis. Fathers commonly disengage from parenting when their initial attempts to take care of their children on their own do not succeed very well and they feel painfully inadequate.

In some cases, these adequacy doubts may be aroused for fathers who were effective and involved parents before the divorce. These fathers believe that they should be active participants in child-rearing and that they have a continuing parenting responsibility after divorce. However, even men who are familiar with the parental role may sometimes feel inadequate and insecure about their ability to care for their children on their own. A capable divorcing father told me, "When I was married I could change my daughter's diapers, bathe her, feed her, everything. It was easy and I enjoyed it. My wife was working full-time and I was an equal coparent. But now that my wife's not around I'm always afraid of doing the wrong thing. It's stupid, I know, but now I can't even do the things I used to do just fine without worrying that I might do something wrong."

Despite such apprehensions and the delimited sex roles that leave many divorced fathers poorly prepared for active parenting, fathers should be encouraged to remain closely involved with their children. When fathers relinquish their parenting role, their children will certainly be affected.

The Adverse Consequences When Father Is Unavailable

When fathers do not take an active role in raising their children after divorce, children are more likely to develop long-term emotional problems. As noted previously, the effects will vary according to the age and sex of the child. In general, however, the effects of fathers' unavailability will be most noticeable in academic, social, and emotional problems—especially depression.

Academic and Social Problems

Research studies have repeatedly shown that children who effectively lose their fathers through divorce do not perform as well in many academic or social dimensions as children who have an emotionally available father. For example, children of absentee fathers have lower grades, score lower on achievement tests, and miss school more often. Boys with absent fathers also score lower on standardized intelligence tests such as the Scholastic Aptitude Test

(S.A.T.) and the Graduate Record Exam. Boys whose fathers show little or no interest in their children achieve lower scores in quantitative subjects and math than boys with present and more actively involved fathers. To take one example, consider the high school S.A.T. test, which measures verbal and quantitative skills on a scale ranging from 200 to 800. Boys whose fathers are absent or uninvolved tend to score significantly lower on the mathematical section than on the verbal (for example, math 400; verbal, 475) compared to boys with an emotionally available father (for example, math 480; verbal, 475). The lower quantitative score reflects a deficiency in abstract thinking ability. The father's absence tends to diminish this conceptual ability in both boys and girls, but the deficit is more pronounced for boys and is most marked when the father departed before the son was five years of age.

In addition to intellectual and academic deficiencies, personality and social problems also trouble father-absent children. Boys without an emotionally responsive father are more dependent and have more difficulty adopting a male sex role than boys with an emotionally available father. For example, some boys who lose their fathers through divorce will have trouble competing successfully with other boys their own age. These boys may be more immature and only play with girls and younger children. Boys who are older when they lose their father often react by rebelling against adult authority. These boys become more aggressive, more impulsive, and harder to discipline.

Although the adverse effects of losing their fathers seem to be greater for sons than for daughters, problems arise for daughters as well. Girls' problems are most likely to become evident when daughters reach adolescence. Teenaged girls who have lost their fathers through divorce will have more difficulty in establishing satisfying love relationships with males. Researchers report that father-absent girls approach males more assertively, become sexually active at a younger age, and have more sexual partners than girls whose fathers are active in their lives.

Unfortunately, these problems with heterosexual relations during adolescence carry over into early adulthood and marriage. Later in life, these girls are likely to have unstable, unsatisfying marriages that end in divorce. Father-absent daughters also tend to select marital partners who are self-centered, immature, and unable to respond to their needs and concerns. Their preconception that men are no good is often confirmed in their choice of marriage partner.

Thus, long-term intellectual, personal, and sex-role problems are associated with the absence of the father for both boys and girls. Does this mean that every child whose father disappears after the divorce will suffer these problems? No, absolutely not—these responses are average. We cannot predict the consequences for any one child; there will always be broad individual differences and variations. Some father-absent children adjust exceptionally well if they have especially competent mothers. These unusually successful single mothers are emotionally available, maintain firm but sensitive discipline, communicate well with their children, and encourage independent mature behavior in them.

There seem to be two types of highly successful single mothers. Some mothers who were very traditional wives and were terrified by the divorce became especially capable single parents. While growing up, these mothers enjoyed a strong relationship with their own fathers, who were nurturing and supportive while also setting high performance standards for them. The other type of highly successful single mother was very independent before the divorce and so is especially capable of providing a well-organized, highly structured household. Nevertheless, although the absence of the father does not necessarily yield long-term problems, there is still a compelling need to ensure fathers' participation in child-rearing after divorce.

Emotional Problems

When fathers disengage from child-rearing after the divorce, children usually feel sad and angry, and many of them will eventually become depressed. These three typical emotional reactions merit a closer examination.

SADNESS. As previously noted, sadness is the predominant initial response to marital disruption of children under eight years of age. Shortly after their father moves out, children may feel very sad, especially if they don't have regular and consistent contact with him. At first, this grief may be openly displayed through emotional pleas such as "I want my daddy. When will my daddy come back?" These children feel weepy, cry a great deal, and have a seemingly insatiable need for physical contact and reassurance. And, later, if the father stays away, these children may become depressed in order to reduce or mask the sharpness of their hurt. This defensive maneuver is an attempt to cope with their sadness and loss.

ANGER. Anger is the predominant initial feeling for older children and adolescents, although all children will experience both anger and sadness. Eight- to twelve-year-old boys are especially angry after a divorce if their father has left them. If the father is not an active parent after the divorce, boys experience a painful loss that they do not want and do not understand.

Boys express this anger by driving their poor mothers and teachers crazy. Many single mothers describe life with their defiant, uncooperative, and obnoxious sons as a war. Day-to-day living can be miserable for both mother and son and this conflict can continue for years. Some of these mothers feel like the helpless victims of their combative sons as they are trapped in an escalating negative cycle in which the son becomes angrier, needier, and harder to control, while the mother becomes increasingly frustrated, depressed, and ineffective. In response to his mother's criticism, the son becomes even more obnoxious and difficult to parent.

Mothers may seek relief from this miserable situation by trying to keep themselves busy from home as much as possible, yet they feel guilty about not being good parents and not spending enough time with their children. The best solution to this hostile entanglement between mother and son is for sons to spend regularly scheduled time with an emotionally available father.

The sadness and anger that children are likely to feel when they lose contact with their father through divorce can be frightening in their intensity and can cause further insecurity over being out of control. However, a more important reaction in children is depression.

DEPRESSION. Boys and girls of all ages who lose their father through divorce face a profound personal loss. This loss of love, which may be exacerbated by receiving less from an overburdened single mother, dramatically lowers self-esteem and results in childhood depression. This depression can be expressed through many different behavioral symptoms and can endure for years.

Childhood depression occurs in response to a perceived or actual loss of love and consists of two essential components. First, losing a parental relationship produces a negative self-image in children. Children feel: "I am not lovable. I am not worthy. There is something wrong with me." The second component of childhood depression is a loss of initiative. The child feels helpless and hopeless, no longer competent to do things well. These children perceive themselves as "losers"—they expect to fail and will not want to take on new challenges or activities. Depression in younger children manifests as a loss of their sense of self-worth or lovableness; older children tend to suffer more from a critical evaluation of their own abilities and from loss of initiative.

Parents may observe signs of depression in their children in any of the following four categories of behavior.

1. *Emotional.* Depressed children feel sad, cry, and look tearful. The sadness that was evident in their initial response to marital disruption continues for at least six months after the separation.
2. *Motivational.* Grades and schoolwork decline as children fail to complete homework assignments and are not motivated to study. In addition they neglect household chores and are less interested in playing and other activities they used to enjoy.
3. *Physical.* Depressed children may lose their appetites or not want to eat as much. Favorite foods are no longer appealing. Children will have vague physical complaints, such as stomach pains, headaches, or just "feeling sick."
4. *Cognitive.* Children will anticipate failure (for example, "I can't do this"). They expect failure in any arena—with friends, in sports, or at school.

Children under nine or ten years of age tend to have more emotional and physical signs of depression; older children tend to have more of the motivational and cognitive symptoms. The symptoms in these four categories comprise the overt signs of depression in children, but they are not the whole story of childhood depression.

Children can also be depressed without showing such relatively obvious symptoms. Many kinds of exaggerated behavior or behavioral problems are attempts by children to mask underlying depression. For example, some children may seek the stimulation of drugs or reckless behavior to ward off the emptiness and boredom of depression. Other children may try to escape depression by becoming apathetic and withdrawing into TV, videos, or music. Perhaps children's most common defense against depression, however, is to escape into agitated motion. School-aged boys particularly may try to cope with the loss of their father through hyperactivity—agitated, heightened activity that is frequently an attempt to ward off the feelings associated with parental loss.

Alarmingly, some estimates suggest that as many as ten percent of the boys in U.S. public schools are being medically sedated for hyperactivity. These boys are prescribed an amphetamine named ritalin that increases activity level for adults but has the reverse effect on prepubescent children. This medication is appropriate and helpful for some active and impulsive boys who have an "attention deficit disorder." If these boys have a longstanding problem in maintaining their focus of attention, ritalin can help them concentrate for longer periods so they can succeed better in school.

However, a large proportion of boys being chemically subdued do not have a cognitively based attention problem. They are simply warding off the pain of depression by escaping into agitated motion. These active and disruptive boys certainly pose a behavior management problem for even the most concerned teachers and parents. However, rather than fostering the child's dependence on medication, it is necessary to address the underlying loss at the source of this heightened activity level (and the lack of effective discipline and the disorganized home environment that usually accompanies this behavior). Whenever parental loss has occurred, parents should first consider whether the child is masking depression before accepting a diagnosis of "attention deficit disorder with hyperactivity" and beginning sedation. Two factors can prevent these defensive maneuvers that inhibit children's growth and ability to adjust. First, children need firm discipline, more adult supervision, and a structured home environment. Second, they need regularly scheduled time with an emotionally responsive father.

Gender Differences in the Effects of Divorce

Significant gender differences are found in every aspect of children's responses to divorce. Before examining differences between boys' and girls' reactions to divorce and absent fathers, we should briefly consider differences in husbands' and wives' perceptions about the divorce.

First, there is normally a poor match between men's and women's description of their divorce. Former spouses do not share perceptions of who initiated the divorce, what was happening in the marriage and in the family before the breakup, or what event precipitated the breakup. Husbands and wives also have different complaints about what was wrong in the marriage.

Women are most likely to complain about men's inability to communicate. Wives wanted their husbands to talk more about themselves and their feelings and to be more affectionate and intimate. Secondarily, divorced wives tend to be dissatisfied because of lack of shared interests and activities. Disturbingly, many women also complain of alcohol-related problems with their husbands and of being physically intimidated by them.

Men have a different list of complaints about the past marriage. Husbands' primary dissatisfaction is that their wives were always complaining and criticizing them. Men often depict their wives as carping and nagging all the time. Although both men and women complain of sexual problems, their concerns are different. Men often complain about the infrequency of sexual relations, whereas women are dissatisfied because they wanted more affection. These differences in perceptions also continue after the divorce, as custodial mothers' reports of the extent of fathers' visitation with the children bear little resemblance to fathers' reports.

Another gender difference concerns later adjustment to divorce. In the years following the breakup, women often adjust better than men, who are at much greater risk of health problems, psychiatric admissions, and accidents. This success, in part, is because women and girls are more effective than men and boys in seeking and receiving emotional support to cope with the stresses of divorce.

In parallel, many researchers also find marked gender differences for children. About ninety percent of all children of divorce reside with a custodial mother. The problems caused by marital conflict, divorce, and life in the care of a single-mother are more pervasive for boys than they are for girls. Boys in single-mother families, in contrast to girls in single-mother families and to children in intact homes, have more long-term adjustment problems. As noted earlier, younger boys tend to be more dependent and help-seeking, whereas older boys are more aggressive and disobedient. Compared to girls, boys in single-mother-headed homes exhibit more behavior problems at school and at home, have more trouble getting along with friends at school, and have poorer school achievement. Two years after the divorce, girls in mother-headed families tend to be as well adjusted as girls in intact two-parent homes. In contrast, there tends to be an increasingly widening gap between the behavior of boys in mother-headed homes and boys in two-parent homes.

How do we account for the fact that boys have more difficulty coping with divorce than girls? Researchers have shown that, following the divorce, parents give less effective discipline to boys, direct more anger and criticism at boys, and provide less nurturing to boys than girls. Let's examine each of these three factors separately.

Why do boys receive less effective discipline than girls following divorce? Researchers have found that parents are more involved in disciplining the same-sex child than the opposite-sex child. That is, daughters tend to be disciplined more by their mothers than their fathers, and sons tend to be disciplined more by their fathers than their mothers. Thus, if the father is not actively involved in parenting after the divorce, the son loses his most important source of discipline. In contrast, because mothers usually retain custody, there is little or no loss of discipline for girls. Mother is there to set and enforce limits for her daughter, just as she has always done, but the father's absence usually means that discipline is inconsistent for boys. This loss contributes to their aggressive and disobedient behavior following the divorce. As we explore in chapter 10, all children adjust better when parents provide effective discipline.

Furthermore, studies have shown that, in addition to receiving less consistent discipline after divorce, boys receive more criticism and anger from both their parents than girls do, although these responses are especially likely to come from mothers. In addition, as we noted in chapter 5, boys are exposed to more parental fighting than girls. Taken together, these factors contribute to sons' lowered self-esteem and problems with aggressive behavior.

The third factor that differentiates how parents respond to boys and girls after divorce is nurturing. As we have seen, boys and girls will both feel anxious and insecure during the time of marital disruption, and children will try to get adults to respond to their increased dependency at this time. For example, children might express this by saying: "Can I sit in your lap?" "Read me one more story." "Why can't I sleep with you tonight?"

However, teachers, mothers, and fathers all respond to girls' increased need for reassurance and affection more readily than they do to boys' need. For instance, teachers readily hold five-year-old girls on their laps and comfort them at school, but these needs are less likely to be met for boys. Similarly, parents touch and hold daughters at home, but do not provide sons with the same affection and reassurance. Our culture's sexual stereotypes deny these needs in boys—they quickly become taboo because they are labeled as being "babyish" or "sissy." However, it is important for parents to recognize that their young sons have the same needs for affection, touching, and caring as their daughters.

At least until adolescence, when mother–daughter conflict often increases, there is more child-rearing stress for single mothers with sons than with daughters. This tendency may also be true in intact families. The 1990 U.S. census revealed that couples are nine percent more likely to stay married if they have sons than if they have daughters. One interpretation of this finding is that mothers with sons are less willing to divorce and raise them alone than mothers with daughters. Also, as we have seen, boys in both intact and divorced homes are less likely to obey their mothers than their fathers. Unfortunate cultural norms encourage boys to be assertive and aggressive, and so it is harder for mothers to nurture and discipline a disobedient and disruptive son. Thus a negative cycle often begins in which sons become more angry toward and demanding of single mothers, and mothers feel increasingly helpless and resentful as their attempts to discipline fail.

Further evidence of the greater difficulty in raising sons after divorce is found in sibling relationships. Researchers find more anger and conflict between sons, and between sons and daughters, than between sisters. Older daughters in divorced homes often take a teaching/caring role with younger sisters and get along with them better. Perhaps these differences occur because boys, on average, are temperamentally more difficult and because girls are socialized to be more cooperative and empathic. For these and other reasons, however, boys need to be effectively disciplined, to be shown consistency and order, and to be nurtured. Single mothers caught in these negative cycles with sons can often be helped by parenting classes that teach them to take control and discipline more effectively. Effective parenting skills are especially necessary to help mothers raising sons on their own to begin to feel in charge and confident. Such skills as learning how to utilize time-out effectively and how to employ natural consequences are essential in this situation.

These gender differences become even more complex, however. In chapter 11, for example, we will see that boys tend to adjust positively to a responsible stepfather, whereas girls struggle with this new addition. Further, the gender differences observed between boys and girls change as children grow into adolescence. Divorce is harder for young boys than girls, but when girls reach adolescence conflict often escalates between single mothers and daughters to match conflict between young sons and mothers. In addition to mother–daughter conflict, adolescent girls are likely to develop problems in dating and heterosexual relations if their father has not been actively involved in their lives. The best solution to all of these problems, for boys and girls at every age, is effective discipline and affectionate caring from both their mothers and their fathers.

Fathering After Divorce

Although some men are very effective fathers after divorce, many others struggle with the role of part-time father. Several styles of fathering are common, but there are several steps that divorced fathers can take to be more involved with their children.

Problematic Fathering Styles

THE IRRESPONSIBLE FATHER. Many view the father as the bad guy and romanticize his new single life. He is characterized as someone having fun, chasing women, and shedding child-rearing demands while the mother has to stay at home and deal with her son's anger because his father has left. Certainly this scenario sometimes occurs. Some fathers are simply irresponsible and do not wish to fulfill their child-rearing responsibilities after divorce.

When this is the case, the children should be made aware of it. Rather than allowing promises of continuing involvement to be broken, mothers and fathers should tell children that their father is leaving and will not be back in any regular or dependable fashion. It is not in the child's best interest to keep alive unrealistic hopes of someday being close to the father. Unfulfilled promises engender lifelong feelings of distrust and disillusion. Although this is a very harsh reality to present to children, it should not be avoided. Too often, the mother inappropriately tries to protect the father or the children from the consequences of the father's behavior by misleading the children.

In a related fashion, some fathers promise involvement with their children but fail to follow through regularly on their commitments. Although infrequent contact is easier for children to adjust to than total rejection, fluctuating or inconsistent visiting patterns are harmful. Parents must be aware that this undependable pattern creates a great deal of suffering when children are repeatedly disappointed. Also, young children's egocentricity makes them assume responsibility for their father's unavailability; they feel that he doesn't see them regularly because they are somehow lacking or unlovable ("There must be something wrong with me or Dad would want to see me"). This type of in-and-out father who promises a relationship but routinely disappoints will often precipitate depression, low self-esteem, and school failure in children. It is heartbreaking to watch as children's attempts to elicit his involvement fail.

When fathers are rejecting or disappointing, mothers must communicate to the child that this is a shortcoming or limitation in the father's ability to love and be a parent; it is not a reflection of the child's basic worth or lovableness. It is essential to stress this repeatedly or children will feel that they were somehow lacking, had some essential defect, or did something wrong that kept father from staying. For boys, in particular, long-term enduring relationships with father surrogates must be found either through organizations like

Big Brothers, the YMCA, or the Boy Scouts or with priests or ministers, family friends, or especially, uncles and grandfathers. Whenever possible, mothers should also try to recruit men as therapists, camp counselors, coaches, and teachers. Mothers raising sons alone should go to great lengths to select teachers who combine clearly defined rules and regularly enforced limits, warmth and affection, and expectations for mature responsible behavior. Permissive or unstructured teachers (and parents) will fail disastrously with these boys.

THE IMMOBILIZED FATHER. A very different kind of father also chooses—but for other reasons—to relinquish contact with his children following the divorce. Most people are not aware of this counterpoint to the irresponsible, abandoning father described previously. Researchers have found another group of fathers who were especially loving and concerned parents before the divorce but found it too painful to continue their involvement with their children afterwards. In some other cases, their former wives had aligned the children with her and against him as the enemy. These mothers often align their daughters against their fathers by enlisting the children as sexual spies ("Who is he with now?").

These otherwise responsible and sensitive fathers are unable to visit their children in another man's home, see their children on a part-time basis with regular leave takings, or tolerate their children's angry and rejecting feelings toward them. Rather than continue to be hurt by these arrangements, these fathers choose to exit from their role as a parent. It is especially hard for children to lose a relationship that had previously been good. Almost every noncustodial father who tries to remain a responsible parent reports repeated frustrations and sorrow caused by visitation. However, fathers can find better ways to cope than withdrawal or abandonment. These concerned but immobilized fathers must find a counselor or support group that appreciates the obstacles they are contending with. With this help, they can manage their sadness and helplessness more effectively and continue to provide the quality parenting they did before the divorce.

When fathers either cannot keep or are uninterested in maintaining their parental relationship, children are faced with a tremendously difficult problem. It is far less difficult to adjust to a change in the frequency of contact with a parent than it is to adjust to the end of a relationship. The termination of a relationship is akin to a death; children must cope with the sadness and helplessness of their loss. Thus, psychological problems are far more likely to develop for the child who entirely loses a relationship with a parent, even if the departing parent and the child were not especially close or involved before the divorce. If the father does exit, the help of a child psychologist or family therapist may ease the child's adjustment to this very difficult loss.

THE UNCERTAIN FATHER. The irresponsible father and the immobilized father are only a minority of divorced men. What about the large majority of fathers, who have become minimally involved in their children's lives after divorce? The main reason that few fathers take an active part in raising their children following divorce is the restrictive sex role. Sadly, many men question whether they have anything important to offer their children and about their competence as a parent. Men often find it hard to nurture and give emotional support to a dependent child, and many men and women seem to believe that children innately belong more to their mothers than to their fathers. This lack of identification with the parental role keeps men from fully participating in child-rearing after divorce. Instead, the responsibility is left to the mother, who is often under a great deal of social pressure to take primary custody of the children, even if she wants to share child-rearing more fully. Fortunately, it is often relatively easy to increase the father's involvement.

In one study, therapists met with fathers for only a few counseling sessions that were aimed at encouraging fathers' continued parental involvement. These therapists helped fathers see that they still had an important role to play in their children's lives and had much to contribute to their development. The therapists also helped them establish concrete plans for visitation and living arrangements that would ensure regular father–child contact. This short-term therapy was tremendously successful. Most of these fathers were still actively involved with their children five years later. This high level of sustained participation is very different from the usual low level of father–child contact. With only a few hours of encouragement, coupled with planning effective strategies for visitation, these men stayed in their children's lives. The benefits of this involvement were clearly reflected in the increased ability of their children to adjust to divorce. The message is clear: Fathers must be encouraged to be actively involved parents after divorce.

Helping Divorced Men Become More Involved Fathers

The inadequacies of traditional child-rearing roles are most evident in post-divorce family relationships, in which most divorced fathers are too distant and mothers are burdened by the overwhelming demands of single parenting. What can be done to provide children with the fathering and mothering they continue to need?

Parents' answers to this question usually cast blame. If you ask divorced mothers why fathers are uninvolved in parenting, a typical reply is, "I've done everything I can to keep him involved with the kids, but he doesn't want anything to do with them. He never has. The kids don't really want to visit him either. They only go because I tell them they must. Actually, they would rather be home with their friends."

In sharp contrast, if you ask divorced fathers why they are disengaged, they predictably respond, "She makes it really hard for me to be with the children. It's little things, like being late whenever I go to pick them up or having them doing something 'more important' than being with me—like going to a birthday party. I don't think she's ever wanted me to have my own relationship with the kids. She believes, like she told the judge, that children just ought to be with their mothers. Even when I tried to do something with the kids when we were married, she would criticize me and tell me the 'right' way to do it. And now I get squeezed the other way, too. My new wife resents the money I send them and tells me that I give in to my ex-wife too easily. After awhile, it just all starts to feel impossible."

Both sides have legitimate concerns, but these radically differing viewpoints mainly reflect poor communication between angry former spouses and the inevitable polarization caused by mutually exclusive and competing child-rearing roles. Such arguments over mothers' and fathers' rights must cease so that their children can have a dependable relationship with both parents that includes frequent, regularly scheduled, and conflict-free access to both their mother and their father. There are many practical ways to achieve this.

Divorcing parents must realize that the most loving gift they can give to their children is permission to be as close to the other parent as to themselves. Parents need to disentangle their own lingering hostility toward the former spouse from the child's need for a continuing relationship with the other parent. Grandparents can help by not taking sides against their former son- or daughter-in-law and, instead, by discouraging both parents from embroiling children in parental battles and painful loyalty conflicts. Friends can support the father's identity as a parent by emphasizing the importance of his contribution to his children's lives and the importance of his children to the quality of his life. A new woman in a man's life needs to support his efforts to remain involved with his children and not interpret this commitment as a threatening tie to his former wife.

Others outside the immediate circle of family and friends can also help. Counselors must help divorcing parents make concrete plans for custody and access arrangements, beginning at the time of separation, that ensure fathers' active participation in parenting. Teachers can reach out to divorced fathers by personally inviting them to attend parent–teacher conferences and other school-related activities and by mailing report cards and school notices to both parents. Employers need to recognize that the most important job for every American is child-rearing and provide the flexible work schedules and on-site daycare facilities that other industrialized nations provide. Family law attorneys must discourage litiginous parents from fighting over children in court; instead they should impress upon clients that whenever one parent "wins" custody or access restrictions on the other, the children lose, not the former spouse. Judges must examine their own sex-role biases, discard myths about the primacy of motherhood, and recognize that children belong equally to their mothers and their fathers.

Although parenting plans must be tailored to fit the circumstances of each family, they must guarantee both parents an active parenting role. If the father prefers to let the mother have primary physical custody, he should receive a generous access schedule that includes overnight stays every week, rather than the alternate weekend visitation scheme that undermines the father–child relationship.

Many fathers recognize, and welcome, their continuing responsibility to care for their children after divorce. However, without the concerted efforts suggested above, many fathers will not be able to assume an effective parenting role on their own. The period of the divorce is the time for everyone to work together and ensure that children will have both a mother and a father after the divorce.

7

Custody, Mediation, and the Courts

Parents must balance two essential needs in determining all custody/access arrangements. First, the continuity of the child's relationship with both parents must be a given. Second, access (visitation) arrangements must be handled in a way that shields children from exposure to marital conflicts. These two goals should provide the principal guidelines for all custody and access arrangements. With these two guiding parameters in mind, parents can establish many different kinds of parenting plans, each with their own strengths and limitations. In most cases, mediation is a far better way to resolve custody disputes than litigation. Nevertheless, because so many custody and access arrangements are decided in court, we begin by briefly reviewing the history of these arrangements.

The History of Custody Determinations

In the 1990s custody adjudication is still in a period of flux. The traditional means of deciding on custody matters are changing, but clear guidelines for today's parents have not yet emerged. Surprising though it may be now, the law once favored fathers as exclusive custodial parents and only later shifted in favor of the mother. The present confusion over custody arrangements arises from another shift as the legal system attempts to find a new middle ground for determining shared responsibility.

Throughout the eighteenth and nineteenth centuries, American and British judges awarded custody solely to the father. This preference was grounded in the economic reality that fathers were better able to provide for the children financially. Court decrees came to romanticize the father's benevolent and nurturing role, by including such assertions as "Only a father's special love for his children can provide. . . ."

Economic and social changes began to influence this legal bias at the beginning of this century. By 1900 the United States had shifted from a farming nation to an industrial society. As a consequence, the extended family of grandparents, uncles, and aunts was replaced by the nuclear family because the labor force became mobile and moved from the farm to factories in the cities. Father became the primary wage-earner in the factory and mother became the primary child care provider in the home. At this point the mother's importance in nurturing and caring for children began to be revered, just as the father's had in the previous century.

By 1900 mothers were seen as the possessors of an inherent nurturing ability ("maternal instinct") that orients them toward children and makes them more effective than fathers in bringing up children. The idea gradually evolved that children suffer irreparable damage if separated from their mothers during the formative "tender years" of early childhood. This tender years doctrine then emerged as the legal basis for supporting the mother as the preferred custodial parent.

From 1900 up to the 1960s, the legal preference for maternal custody prevailed, and the father was viewed as a breadwinner with no direct child-rearing role. The mother was granted custody of children, and the father was issued alternate weekend visitation rights and required to pay alimony and child-support to "the family."

These arrangements did not work well. They discouraged fathers from an active part-time parenting role and overloaded mothers with the demands of single parenting. Furthermore, when fathers do not have an active relationship with their children, they are less likely to keep up child-support payments, so that an additional burden falls on mothers and children. These failings, the growth of the women's movement, growing recognition that the tender years doctrine is a social bias rather than a biological predisposition, the rapid adoption of no-fault divorce in most states, and research findings on the positive effects of father's involvement have all led to a new era in custody and access arrangements.

In the past fifteen years, the tender years doctrine has been replaced with "best interests of the child" statutes. Although it is difficult, if not impossible, for courts to determine what is truly in the child's best interest, this approach supported fathers' more active role in child-rearing and addressed the growing concern that the previous maternal bias constituted sex discrimination. In the 1980s, these factors led courts toward joint custody arrangements as a potentially better answer to the complex and painful issues of custody determination. Without question, joint custody has provided a beneficial new middle ground that encourages both parents' participation in raising their children. However, there is no panacea to the significant problems that divorce arouses, and joint custody will not work for many families—especially if parents are combative. Below, we will evaluate the pros and cons of this frequently misunderstood arrangement, as well as the effects on children of other custody and access schedules.

Joint Custody and Other Alternatives

Throughout this book I make suggestions and recommendations for divorcing parents based on well-documented research results. Much of this research on children and divorce was not available even a few years ago. Although we now know a great deal about the different factors that cause healthy versus problem-ridden adjustment to divorce, we are just beginning to learn about the effects of different custody and access arrangements on children. Some research in this area has been completed and further studies are underway, but the questions about the effects of different plans are only partially answered. In this section I share the information and guidelines that are now available, but parents should know that there is less factually supported information in this area than in others covered in this book.

Furthermore, there cannot be easy answers to the profound dilemmas of custody determination when the stakes are so high. Parents must begin this process knowing that they cannot find a perfect parenting plan that will not be accompanied by additional problems. There is no established formula for divorcing couples—what has worked well for one family may cause problems for another.

Thus parents need to discuss, compromise, and tailor specific plans to fit their own individual circumstances. As years go by, parents will also need to revise these plans to ensure that they continue to meet the changing needs of their children. In most cases, a divorce mediator can offer parents a great deal of help in establishing effective parenting plans and resolving custody disputes.

Finally, before going on I must acknowledge one more issue. The language often used in child custody statutes is problematic and often threatens parental power and identity. The terms "custody," "visitation," "sole custody," and even "joint custody" connote ownership of children and reflect the adversarial court process from which these terms have been derived. For example, children do not leave their homes with their mothers to visit their fathers. His children are equally at home at his house; they are not visitors who really belong to their custodial mothers, as this language suggests. In 1991 British courts acknowledged the power of language to invalidate a parent's role and discarded these weighted terms. Instead of making custody and visitation orders, British courts now use more neutral terms and make a "contact order" and a "residence order." American courts are also beginning to change and terms such as "residential parent" instead of custodial parent and "access parent" instead of visiting parent are coming into use in some states. Unfortunately, these new terms have not yet been widely incorporated and they do not exist in most court decrees. There is great significance in this choice of language, however, and American courts should give priority to adopting better terms.

Joint Legal and Physical Custody

Since 1980 many states have enacted legislation that encourages frequent and continuing contact with both parents. "Joint legal custody," in which children have a primary residence but parents share responsibility for making important decisions, is often the preferred alternative and is currently awarded in about eighty percent of divorce cases. Joint custody is a beneficial new approach that works well for most cooperative parents, and often succeeds when parents cannot communicate well with each other but can successfully shield children from parental conflict. However, this arrangement has been too often erroneously applied to embittered and embattled couples for whom it fails disastrously. Joint custody has also been widely misunderstood.

The principal misunderstanding about joint custody is the confusion between joint legal custody (shared responsibility for important decisions regarding children) and joint physical custody (visitation or access schedules). Joint custody does not mean a fifty-fifty split in which former spouses are bound by law to equally share the time spent with their children. Nor do children have to move between two homes on alternate weeks, or for alternate six-month stays, or any other rigid enforcement of equal time. Joint legal custody simply legally defines both parents as having equal power and authority in making decisions affecting their children (for example, education, medical care, religious affiliation, general welfare). By giving parents this equal role, joint legal custody validates both the father's and the mother's continued parental role and encourages both parents to remain actively involved in the children's lives.

Within this joint legal framework, parents can then make any physical custody plans (access arrangements or visitation schedules) they wish. Some parents may wish to fully share child care on a fifty-fifty basis; most will not. Although many different coparenting arrangements are possible, the guiding principle in all determinations should be continuity of child–parent relationships and protecting children from exposure to parental conflict.

Among the different kinds of coparenting, researchers have found that residential parents with primary physical custody (either sole custody or joint custody) are more satisfied with living arrangements than noncustodial or outside parents with whom the children only visit. When some type of shared parenting arrangements have been made and children spend a significant amount of time in both households, the arrangement usually falls into one of three different patterns of coparenting.

First, about one fourth of coparenting couples maintain a cooperative relationship with each other. These parents are capable of working together in the child's best interest and they successfully isolate their conflicts with each other from their functions as parents. These cooperative parents also make plans for their children, discuss children's problems, attempt to enforce similar rules between households, and back up each other's parenting. Joint legal custody and some type of shared parenting are ideal for these harmonious couples. These parents disprove the widely held myth that an unworkable marriage can only result in an unworkable parenting relationship.

Second, approximately one third of shared parenting couples are disengaged from each other but not combative. These parents seldom talk to their former spouses and do not attempt to coordinate activities and rules between households. However, they manage the logistics of visitation with little conflict and children do not see their parents argue or undermine each other. In most cases, these parents have made plans to exchange the children at times and places at which they do not have to see each other or interact (for example, at school, not at home). It seems that children often adjust well in these families in which parents may go a year or longer hardly speaking to each other. Research suggests that parents are more likely to be successfully disengaged from each other—in effect, parallel parents—if children are older. It may be harder for parents to achieve this neutrality if children are under the age of six.

Coparenting arrangements are ideally suited for cooperative parents and seem to work well for most disengaged but noncombative parents. However, in the third category, about one third of coparenting divorced couples are in conflict with each other, and shared parenting arrangements pose significant problems for their children. These parents do not cooperate or communicate well, and their conflicts spill over into their parenting. They argue in front of the children when they make exchanges, threaten to take the children away from each other, accuse the other parent of undermining them, and often try to handle their problems by repeated litigation. Research suggests that family size may be one factor related to this higher level of interparental conflict. Parents find it easier to avoid conflict if they have only one child, but discord seems especially difficult to avoid if they have three or more children.

Shared parenting plans can be very damaging to children of embattled parents. Researchers have found that children who shared more days each month with embittered and embattled parents are significantly more likely to be described by their parents as depressed, withdrawn, and uncommunicative; they are also more likely to have somatic symptoms such as headaches, stomachaches, and sleep disturbances, and aggressiveness. What parenting plans are better suited to these combative families?

In these families, shared parenting arrangements should not be established. Instead, sole legal custody and primary physical custody should be given to the parent who provides the children with the least contested access to the other parent. That is, preference should be given to the parent who is most willing to allow ample and unconflicted visitation to the other parent ("friendly parent" provisions). If neither parent is more cooperative, primary physical custody should be given to the more effective parent.

The courts usually rely on psychological evaluations to make both of these determinations. If neither parent is evaluated as more adept as a parent or better at facilitating the child's relationship with the other parent, two options can be followed. Children can be placed with the same-sex parent and given generous visitation schedules with the other parent. Or, in a few cases, sole legal and primary physical custody can be given to each parent in alternate years. This allows both parents to remain involved, but they do not have to cooperate or interact extensively about decisions for the child. Unfortunately, these alternate-year transitions may be harmful for some children, but less so than leaving children exposed to their parent's continuing battle.

Thus, I encourage most cooperative parents, and disengaged parents who can contain their conflicts, to establish joint legal custody of their children with some type of shared parenting arrangements, although not necessarily equal-time visitation arrangements. Joint custody serves the goal of working for the best interest of the child. Joint custody helps assuage children's sadness, loneliness, and rejection by increasing their access to both parents.

When parents can provide continuity of relationships without exposing children to parental power struggles, many different physical access plans can be successful. Often, divorcing parents become too focused on the number of hours the child spends with each parent each week and thus miss the more important point that the access schedules themselves are less important than the degree of tension and parental conflict in children's lives. The interparental attitude of cooperation or hostility is more important to children's adjustment than the specific schedule. With this in mind, let's review the different potential visitation or access schedules.

Access Schedules

EQUAL TIME. Some divorcing parents want to share equal time with their children, although this alternative has not been common in the past. However, if the father is willing to accommodate his work schedule and wants equal time with the children, this request will often be granted if the judge believes it is in the child's best interest. There are three different types of equal-time arrangements: split week, alternating years, and shared home.

Split-Week Arrangements. A common and workable equal-time arrangement is for the child to alternate between the parental homes each week, with three and a half days at each. The major concern with this access schedule has been the potentially negative effects on children of repeated separations from the parent they consider their main provider of care and love. This view arises from the belief that children form a primary bond, which must not be broken, to one parent. However, a growing body of evidence suggests that children can form multiple attachments to a hierarchy of caretakers and can adjust very well to a split-week visitation schedule. Evidently, children form primary attachment bonds to more than one person, and a separation from one parent is not so stressful when followed by a reunion with the other. The strength of this shared access arrangement is that it allows children to maintain a close relationship with both parents and prevents them from worrying about the disruption of their relationship with the noncustodial parent.

The drawbacks of this arrangement are the increased number of transitions and reduced day-to-day consistency in the child's life. Some children can readily manage transitions that accompany equal-time arrangements; however, some children find them too disruptive and require the stability of a more central residence. Parents must tailor access arrangements to fit the specific temperament and needs of each individual child (and remember that their child's needs will change over time).

When will the split-week arrangement fail and when will it succeed? This arrangement is ideal for cooperative and mutually supportive former spouses. Because this arrangement requires parental cooperation, it should not be adopted if it will increase children's exposure to parental conflict. Joint physical custody and equal-time arrangements will be problematic for all children whenever parents cannot refrain from fighting with each other, when they regularly criticize the other parent to the children, or when they pressure children to take sides or choose between parents. That is, shared parenting arrangements will not succeed unless hostile former spouses can separate the marital dimension of their relationship from the parental dimension, contain their conflicts, and shield children from parental wrangling. Finally, in order for split-week arrangements to work, the child must have the flexibility and resiliency to make frequent transitions and adjust to two different households. Some children can do this readily; others cannot.

Despite favorable research findings, joint physical custody has received considerable negative press in the early 1990s, mainly because it has been overprescribed and too many combative couples have been pressured to adopt it—to the detriment of their children. If parents cannot agree to avoid each other or interact with some reasonably low level of conflict, equal-time arrangements will be harmful to children. If tensions between parents are chronically high and children are going to be exposed to continuous litigation, sole legal custody is usually preferable. As noted previously, sole legal custody and primary residence should be given to the most cooperative parent, the most capable caregiver, or the same-sex parent. Too often, the difficult decision on a primary residence has been avoided by establishing an equal-time arrangement. This result keeps parents from feeling they have "lost," but it does not work for children.

In order for the split-week arrangement to succeed, parents must also live near each other and the child must continue to attend the same school. The split-week arrangement does not usually work for young children; it is much better suited to children seven and older. School-aged children are oriented toward fairness, and this equally shared visitation arrangement will make sense to them. As children reach ten to twelve, it is usually helpful to let them participate in choosing the pattern of movement between the two parental homes, rather than imposing a visitation schedule on them. This suggestion follows from the general principle that, as children grow older, parents should give them more control over access arrangements whenever possible. Older children usually benefit from being able to participate in decisions about living arrangements. However, in families with high parental tensions and loyalty conflicts, this involvement will only create anxiety and intensify conflicts for children. Finally, most adolescents need a safe harbor, and they often choose a primary residence, usually with the same-sex parent.

Alternate-Year Arrangements. If parents can successfully shield children from their conflicts but do not live near each other, parents may establish an alternate-year arrangement for school-aged children. For example, the child might live with the mother the first year, and then move to the father's home the second year. Sometimes adolescents choose to alternate between parental homes every two years. Although children have to change schools every year or two, adjustment is much easier for many children than losing a primary relationship with one parent. Each year, children should have frequent and regularly scheduled time with the parent they are not living with— for example, at Christmas and spring breaks, and eight to ten weeks each summer.

Although the alternate-year arrangement does not require as much interparental contact as the split-week schedule, the parents must also be able to cooperate—or at least remain neutral or disengaged from each other—for this plan to work. Joint physical custody and equal-time, shared-visitation arrangements work best when former spouses actively support each other as parents. However, they will fail when they only increase children's exposure to parental battles. In addition, they will not work for children who are shy, who make friends and warmup to new situations slowly, or who need more stability and routine in their lives.

A common concern of parents about equal-time and other shared parenting arrangements is whether children will have difficulty in adjusting to two households with different rules and schedules. Several studies suggest that, by school age, children can adjust well to alternating between dissimilar parental homes as long as there is consistency within each home. In order for this arrangement to succeed, parents must follow several guidelines:

1. Cooperate and support each other concerning the children, or at least be able to shield children from parental tensions;

2. Establish a predictable schedule for alternating between residences that young children can count on and plan for (some older children can have more flexible schedules, but predictable routines are usually best);

3. Ensure consistency and predictability of the rules within each of the two parental homes. Children adjust well when there are clearly defined but different rules between the two households on such practices as bedtimes, mealtimes, and acceptable behavior. Children have difficulty when the rules and expectations are not clearly laid out and reliably enforced by each parent in each respective home.

One day Rob returned home from work to find that his wife, Clair, and his seven-year-old son, Robby, had packed their things and moved out. Clair had left a note saying that she was sorry, but she couldn't stay in the marriage any longer. She informed Rob that she was moving to a nearby city and taking their son with her. Rob was furious at his wife and determined to get his son back.

The next six months were confusing and painful for everyone. Rob and Clair had moments when reconciliation seemed possible, but Clair was becoming increasingly interested in another man and Rob could not forgive her for walking out. Things were tough for Robby, too. He was very upset about moving away from his father and often felt sad and tearful. Even though it was hard for Clair to see Robby miss his father so much, she still believed that young children should live with their mothers. Rob disagreed and thought that Robby should be with him. He had always been a very involved parent, and it was clear to him that he could provide greater stability in Robby's life than Clair could. For the divorce settlement, both parents had hired lawyers and psychologists to argue that each was the better parent and should have primary physical custody of Robby.

The judge quickly assessed the family situation. Both Rob and Clair were fit parents who could provide Robby with secure and loving homes. The judge hoped to be able to keep both of these concerned parents in their child's life and thought that joint legal custody with an alternate-year, shared visitation schedule could succeed. Although both parents felt they were losing with this arrangement, Robby stood to gain the most. The judge suspended further hearings until Rob and Clair attempted to resolve their dispute through a court-ordered divorce mediator.

After several sessions with the mediator, both parents relinquished their opening positions and agreed to a shared parenting plan. They agreed to share joint legal custody of Robby. Robby's mother would have primary physical custody of him the first year, and he would be enrolled in a local school where his mother lived. Robby would spend two long weekends a month, Christmas vacation, spring vacation, and eight weeks in the summer with his father. After one year, Robby would move back to his father's home, enroll in school there, and have the same visitation schedule with his mother as he had with his father.

Although the rules were a little different at his mother's than at his father's, Robby knew what was expected of him at each home. Robby's parents were also able to let him know that they loved him and wanted him very much. Although Rob remained angry at Clair for leaving him and trying to take Robby away, he knew that Robby loved his mother and missed her when they were apart. Although Rob was particularly sure that he could never trust Clair again, Rob and Clair were able to separate their personal conflicts with each other from their parenting relationship with Robby. As a result, Robby thrived. The sadness and withdrawal that were evident in Robby's behavior when his parents separated went away as he saw that he could remain close and involved with both his parents. Six years after the divorce, this shared parenting arrangement and Robby's positive adjustment were both still continuing.

Shared House. Some media attention has been given to the situation in which children remain in the same house and their divorced parents periodically move in and out. This visitation arrangement is not suitable for most families on a long-term basis and is so rare that it hardly bears mention. Unfortunately, however, this situation has been used at times to ridicule the concept of joint custody. This prejudice reflects the common confusion over joint legal custody (which encourages both parents' continuing role in the child's life) versus access schedules (which are flexible).

Primary Physical Custody to One Parent

Parents can also establish joint legal custody without adopting the equal-time living arrangements described above. In most cases, parents will want the mother to retain primary physical custody and the father to take an active part-time parenting role. Several different living arrangements are possible when one parent (either father or mother) assumes primary physical custody.

FATHER CUSTODY. In recent years, increasing attention has been given to fathers who seek custody. However, the increased number of men who want custody reflects the increased number of divorces, not an increased percentage of fathers seeking custody. Approximately nine out of ten children of divorce still end up living with their mothers, but when fathers seek primary physical custody they obtain it approximately half the time. Fathers who seek primary physical custody are more likely to be the parents of school-aged and adolescent children than of preschoolers and younger children.

What are the effects on children of living with their father? Researchers have found that children living with their custodial fathers are as well adjusted as those living in their mother's custody. Just as with mothers, child adjustment depends on the father's ability to parent effectively (that is, to provide nurturance, effective discipline, and an orderly household routine) and on his ability to support and encourage the child's relationship with the mother.

Perhaps the most important research finding about maternal versus paternal custody is the interaction between custodial status and the gender of the children. Although only a few studies have been conducted, researchers have consistently found that school-aged children tend to be better adjusted when they live with the same-sex parent. Both boys and girls have more aggressive behavior problems and lower self-esteem when they are living with the opposite-sex parent. However, sons in father-custody homes are also less communicative and affectionate, perhaps as a result of less exposure to female expressiveness. On average, however, boys tend to adjust better than girls in father-custody homes, and girls tend to adjust better than boys in mother-custody homes. If both the mother and the father want primary physical custody, and equal-time, alternate visitation is not satisfactory, parents should consider this same-sex advantage along with other variables noted later in this chapter. A continuing relationship between a child and the same-sex parent seems to be very important, especially when we recall that most divorce researchers find that boys have more adjustment problems than girls. This difference may be largely attributable to the fact that most boys live with their mothers after divorce.

Parents should consider this same-sex advantage in their custody deliberations. However, an even more important finding is that, regardless of which parent has primary physical custody, child adjustment is determined by the parenting ability of the primary caregiver. In both mother- and father-custody families, children of both sexes are best adjusted when parents are affectionate, set clear rules and regulations, and encourage extensive verbal give-and-take. These effective child-rearing practices are elaborated in chapter 10.

MATERNAL CUSTODY. Because most divorced fathers do not seek primary physical custody, about ninety percent of children live with their mothers. Most parents still want the mother to have primary physical custody and the father to establish a schedule for being with their children. However, many of these parents should also establish joint legal custody in order to encourage the father's parental participation and financial support after divorce. Within this joint legal custody framework, the mother has primary physical custody and parents establish a schedule for fathers to be with their children that fits their particular circumstances. These visitation schedules or parenting plans should be established based on some general guidelines.

General Guidelines for Living Arrangements

REGULARITY. Although spontaneity and flexibility are usually appealing, they do not work well in custody matters. A formal schedule that provides specific details about when the child will be with each parent is essential. Schedules minimize parental conflicts because they enable fathers to tell their children when they will see them next without first having to check with mothers, and they ensure that mothers know what will happen without having to ask fathers about their plans. On the other hand, parenting plans must also have some flexibility to meet the changing needs of children and parents. Parents may wish to include a provision in their divorce decree establishing that the parenting plan will be reviewed periodically and that the agreement can be changed with the consent of both parents.

Children function best within a consistent and predictable daily routine, and this regularity is especially important in the aftermath of divorce. Children will be more secure if they know with certainty and in advance which parent they will be staying with each day, and when and where they will see the other parent next. The access schedule that parents agree upon should be carefully presented to the children so that they clearly understand when they will be with each parent. Parents can help children remember when they will be with the other parent by drawing the schedule for them on their own calendar, which they can hang in their room. Whenever the agreed-upon schedule cannot be met, children must be notified in advance of the changes. Erratic visitation schedules that children cannot depend upon are always highly problematic.

Thus, if four-year-old Susie says, "Daddy, I miss Momma, I want to go," the father can respond, "I know you miss Momma sometimes when you come to stay with me. It would feel good to be with her now. But today is Wednesday and that is our time together. Let's go look at your calendar together and you can see that Momma will pick you up tomorrow morning at 8:00 A.M. You can be with her then and tell her how much you missed her."

CONSISTENCY AND FAMILIARITY. In a related vein, parents should try to keep as many factors as possible constant in their child's life during and immediately after the parental separation. Change is stressful. Teachers, babysitters, neighbors, and school companions can all provide an important source of continuity and stability for children while they are coping with the changes at home. Parents should do what they can to avoid changes in a child's routine and environment. New schools and neighborhoods are sometimes necessary after divorce, but they demand further adjustment and accommodation. Whenever possible, parents should minimize changes in children's lives and know that familiarity and stability will be comforting.

In addition, children require their own sense of place. Every child must have at least one space in each parent's home that belongs only to them. At the very least, this space can be only a box or shelf. Parents can further enhance the children's sense of belonging by putting their name on it and keeping their shelf, room, bed, closet, or cubby hole just for them.

FREQUENCY. If the mother has assumed primary physical custody, the more time the father spends with the children, the better. Research studies show that more frequent time with the father is associated with greater intimacy in father–child relations, greater satisfaction for the child during visits, and more effective control over the children by their fathers. Thus fathers should see their children at least once a week, if possible.

Visitation works best when it is frequent and routine. The all-too-common visitation pattern of alternate weekends should be avoided because it is not enough time for the parent and child to know each other. Visitation days for noncustodial fathers usually do not work very well. It is stressful for fathers to handle children for eight hours in an artificial setting in which father and child do not know what to do with each other. Researchers emphatically hear that children of all ages are frustrated and dissatisfied with this very limited contact. Time spent with noncustodial fathers should include regularly scheduled overnight stays and weekends. This arrangement is essential because it allows noncustodial fathers to include children in the daily routines and activities of living (grocery shopping, running errands, visiting friends, cooking dinner). Longer visits will permit these more real-life interactions and help prevent the unsatisfying emphasis on entertainment that characterizes the visits between some noncustodial fathers and their children. (Joint custody works, in part, because this entertaining mode of visitation stops.) Telephone and letter contact should also be maintained between these visits.

One schedule that works well for many divorced families is for noncustodial fathers to have the children live in his home two long weekends each month, beginning after school Thursday and ending Monday morning when the children are dropped off at school. When living with the father includes weekday school nights, fathers are more involved in children's homework, friends, and school. This schedule also creates an arena for the family activities of preparing dinner, engaging in bedtime routines, and getting ready for school. By contrast, only superficial entertainment activities result when fathers see children on Saturdays and Sundays. In addition to these longer weekends, the noncustodial father may also schedule a weekly supper, alternate holidays such as Thanksgiving, Christmas, and birthdays, two weeks at Christmas, a week at spring break, and eight weeks or so in the summer. With less time, children and fathers will not get to know each other and father–child contact will become unrewarding for both. This is why so many father–child relationships wither in the first few years after the divorce.

Finally, with rights come responsibilities. Noncustodial parents must not only seek significant time with their children, but they must follow through and provide this parenting. Children should not be taken away from their primary caretaker only to be cared for by grandparents, a new spouse, babysitters, or daycare workers. Parents who seek more extensive time with their children must be willing to alter their personal priorities and work schedules so they can provide this parenting personally.

THE CHILD'S CONTROL OVER ACCESS TO PARENTS. Children cope better when they feel they have some control over when they see their parents. Children who live with their mother but can bicycle, walk, or take a bus to their father's when they want are most satisfied with visitation arrangements. As we have seen, divorce brings about feelings of helplessness or powerlessness in most children that lower their self-esteem and sense of mastery in the world. If children can exert some control over their visitation schedule, they can cope more effectively with the divorce. Although parents cannot always give children the access schedules they want, parents should listen to what they would like and try to accommodate their preferences as much as circumstances will allow.

In most divorcing families, the father will move out of the family residence and the mother will obtain primary physical custody of the children. Because of economic constraints, many fathers initially move back to their own parents' home. Fathers without custodial living arrangements often move three to five times within the first five years after separation, with disastrous effects on visitation.

Whenever possible, departing fathers should plan their initial move carefully and establish a more permanent residence. Visitation for noncustodial parents can also be enhanced if, at the time of the initial breakup, the noncustodial parent actively involves children in making a new home together so that children feel included rather than abandoned. And, as noted previously, fathers should try to establish their new homes near their former wives so that it is easier for children to see him, maintain the same peer friendships, and retrieve belongings without involving the other parent. Only children who have such easy bicycling or walking access to both their parents' homes say they see each parent "almost enough."

COMINGS AND GOINGS. Visitations, which require children to regularly leave one parent for the other, are difficult times for every family member and must be approached thoughtfully. The parent who is left can have many different reactions: sadness at seeing the child leave, anger toward the former spouse as past conflicts are aroused, or relief over the temporary respite from parental responsibilities. Whatever their feelings, parents who are left behind need to reassure children that they will be fine while the children are gone and that the children can enjoy their visit with the other parent without worrying. Parents who are left can also say that they are pleased the child has the opportunity to spend time with the other parent, but that they will be happy to welcome the child back. In other words, children regularly need overt spoken permission to leave the custodial parent and to feel close to the other parent. Except in extreme circumstances, frequent contact helps children. If you show confidence about visiting, your child will have confidence, too.

The parent the child is going to visit should not necessarily expect the child to feel close to or be happy to see him or her at first. There often needs to be a warming-up period for getting to know each other again. The first night of a visit is usually the most difficult for children, and parents should not be upset or feel rejected if a child is testy or shy. Avoid planning a flurry of activities to entertain the child. Instead, the best way to respond to a child's initial visit is to ease the transition for both parent and child by planning low-key shared activities. For example, parent and child can prepare dinner together, take an after-dinner walk or bicycle ride, and end the evening by reading bedtime stories together. Although at first children may protest that they only want to watch TV, they will soon welcome the more personal contact of reading, painting, or just doing everyday activities together.

Parents and children who see each other infrequently risk losing their potential intimacy and rapport. It is hard to begin visits after a parent and child have been apart, and it is especially hard to end them. To avoid this awkwardness or heartache, too many parents artificially prepare a flurry of activities. "Disneyland daddies" entertain their children—they are not being with them— and the activities are painful for all. Children are relieved if parents can openly acknowledge their difficult feelings about coming and going and communicate to children that it is acceptable to have them. In addition, as noted in chapter 6, successful visitation depends on the father's ability to constructively manage his own feelings of sadness and powerlessness.

Parents and children both need quiet, unstructured time in which they can begin to find each other again. Furthermore, parents and children often do not become as close as they could because they do not talk together well. If children happen to express problems or concerns, mothers sometimes reassure too quickly and fathers sometimes ignore their concerns or become angry about their complaints. Much more closeness could develop if parents would not feel guilty or inadequate about their child's problems and, instead, simply listen. Noncustodial parents must also institutionalize family traditions that permit real communication between parent and child, such as family councils and bedtime rituals with quiet time for conversation. Without such efforts for genuine emotional relatedness, relationships become superficial and visitation drops off. Fathers who want to foster this emotional connection with their children, but who don't know how to provide it because they never received it themselves, can find help. The capacity to establish more meaningful, emotional contact with your children can be learned and understanding mentors can be found.

AGE OF CHILDREN. Although I suggest some visitation schedules that can be arranged for children of different ages, I want to emphasize again that many other options are available that could work better for your children. The schedule that works well for some children may be a disaster for others.

Several short visits per week are better than a few longer visits for infants, who need such regularity. Fathers must be actively involved in feeding, bathing, soothing, and changing the baby. Even though, in most cases, the mother or new wife probably can do these things more skillfully at first, fathers should not give in to fears of inadequacy that keep them from caring for their babies. If others continually correct such fathers or take care of their babies for them, these fathers will never really feel like their children are their own. Fathers need to set limits and say "no, thank you". It is also essential that noncustodial fathers spend time alone with their baby or very young child.

Children under four years of age should not be separated from their primary caretaker for very long. A separation of two or three days is a long time for young children to be away from their primary caregiver. An overnight visit with the noncustodial parent every third or fourth night or the weekend, bolstered by a telephone call every other night, works well for many families. Preschoolers, in particular, need familiar routines and consistent schedules.

School-aged children can tolerate much longer separations, can handle more flexible schedules, and need more time with both parents. Children six to seven years old and older can comfortably alternate between living in the mother's and father's homes every third or fourth day, and extended weekends and overnights during the school week can work well. Access schedules must be arranged to accommodate school and other activities.

Preteens can handle longer visits, and more time with the same-sex parent often becomes important. As children reach midadolescence, by age fifteen to sixteen in particular, they will often want to live with the same-sex parent. Parents should anticipate this preference and accommodate it when possible. In general, adolescents should be important participants in determining visitation plans and living arrangements. Their wishes should be heard and responded to if possible, although access arrangements should not interfere with school, peers, and employment.

TAKING CHARGE. Parents should expect children to test their limits within the new family arrangements. Children are often angry after divorce and attempt to play one parent against the other. Eight- to eleven-year-old boys, in particular, are very angry after divorce, and they can quickly make a visiting father feel guilty and lose interest in visiting. After the divorce, some children will say "I don't want to see you," or claim they would rather be with the other parent. Unfortunately these manipulations are especially successful in distancing noncustodial fathers, who may already feel rejected, guilty, or insecure in their relationships with their children.

Valid complaints from children should be heard, but children should not have the power to decide whether their parent–child relationship will continue. Parents should not let children choose whether to spend time with the noncustodial parent or to have a continuing relationship. The continuity of relations should be presented to the child as a fact. While angry and hurt feelings should be discussed, they should not be used to jeopardize a parental relationship. Sadly, too many fathers overreact to their children's angry rejection and give up their parenting role. Children suffer when they lose the parent they are angry with, and they suffer even more when they are allowed to exert too much control over adult relationships and drive a parent away.

Finally, we have already seen that children are almost certain to develop longterm adjustment problems if their parents continually battle each other in court. The two issues that most frequently bring about court battles are child support payments and the visitation schedules we have been discussing. Below, the final section examines these two problems and encourages parents to utilize a divorce mediator and settle their differences outside of the courtroom whenever possible.

Resolving Disputes Through Mediation

The two traditional but ineffective ways that people respond to conflicts could be characterized as "fight" or "flight." A more creative and satisfying way to resolve most disputes is through mediation. In almost all states, the law gives parents the opportunity to work out their own custody or parenting plans with the help of a neutral mediator. If the two parents can agree on a custody plan, the judge will almost always accept that plan. If parents will not mediate or cannot agree during mediation, the judge will decide for them. While so much of the divorce process feels out of parents' rightful control, mediation offers them the opportunity to decide their own destinies. Let's look more closely at what mediation is and is not.

Mediation is a cooperative way for divorcing couples to resolve their conflicts during and after divorce. A skilled mediator is a neutral professional with knowledge of family law, child psychology, and negotiation techniques. The mediator helps divorcing families clearly define the issues in dispute and reach agreements that are in the best interests of the family. The mediator does this by guiding the communication process so that a rational discussion can take place, everyone has a chance to be heard, and conflicts are discussed one at a time. The mediator does not take sides, assign blame, or make decisions for divorcing couples. Instead, the mediator tries to help parents understand the needs of children, reach agreements that are in the children's best interests, and develop a cooperative parenting relationship. Although the mediator may offer suggestions and help couples develop parenting plans, the final agreement is up to the parents.

Mediation is not marital counseling or psychotherapy. Its purpose is not to help divorcing couples reconcile, but to help families resolve divorce-related issues and reach successful parenting agreements. Similarly, mediation is not a substitute for an attorney. Most parents will still wish to have an attorney help them understand the law, make informed agreements, and write up the final agreement. The mediator focuses on helping couples reach their own agreements and, unlike the attorney, does not represent one party.

Just as joint custody is not a panacea, problems and limitations are also associated with mediation. The process will not work for everyone. Participants do not have to like or trust one another, but they must be willing to work together in good faith to try to find solutions that will be fair to all family members. When one party "wins" settlements, further conflict and litigation inevitably follow and only creates more problems for children.

Mediation is much more likely to fail when either of the parents is physically violent, addicted to drugs or alcohol, or highly dependent on the child for happiness. Couples also tend to end up back in court when one party reluctantly acquiesces to a custody plan during mediation. Finally, the success of mediation is very dependent on whether the attorney's attitude toward mediation is "resolve it out of court" or "just go through the motions."

Thus, some cases must be settled in court. For the majority of families, however, mediation is by far the best alternative for resolving the complex problems that divorce creates. When parents settle disputes in court, the acrimony, bitterness, and distrust between parents are always exacerbated by the adversarial court process. In most cases, the resulting hatred endures for decades. Children suffer tremendously when they see their parents fighting in court, and they are hurt by the interparental hostility that remains for years afterward. In addition to these emotional benefits for parents and children alike, mediated settlements are far less expensive than court battles. And mediated agreements are usually more flexible than court-ordered solutions because they can be changed by mutual consent, rather than having to be filed with the court. Thus, divorcing parents are strongly advised to make sincere efforts to resolve their disputes through mediation before embarking on the highly disruptive, adversarial court process.

The two most common arenas of dispute are child custody and child support, and mediation can play a very constructive role in helping parents resolve these conflicts.

Child Custody Disputes

Very often one parent wants to renegotiate custody or visitation arrangements that have already been handed down. Custody changes are often sought after one party has remarried, and many custody changes are prompted by fathers who seek joint legal custody even though the mother retains primary physical custody. (Mothers often view these latter custody challenges as criticism of their caregiving.) Parents should know that it is easier to establish joint custody and/or equal-time visitation arrangements at the time of the initial divorce decree than it is to change sole custody declarations later on. However, the court will often respond favorably to requests by the noncustodial parent for greater access to the child.

When parents disagree over custody and visitation arrangements, the court often will encourage or mandate them to try to resolve their differences through a divorce mediation program. As noted, these mediation programs are very effective in resolving such disputes in a way that minimizes distress for children. Lengthy, expensive, and polarizing court battles and the stresses associated with psychological evaluations can often be avoided. Parents can fight over money and property in court, but it is never in the children's best interest for parents to fight over children. The adversarial court process dramatically increases parental conflict and distrust and translates directly into additional adjustment problems for children.

Statistics vary, but about fifteen percent of divorcing parents are not able to compromise with each other or end their legal battles. They continue to fight in court over custody of the children and, at times, even try to bar the other parent from seeing the child. Although a minority of such parents are appropriately trying to place needed limits on a disturbed parent's involvement, many are enacting their own personal conflicts with each other through the children. When one parent tries to win sole custody, children usually lose, not the other parent. Litigious parents who are embroiled in continuing legal battles over their children have the most troubled and maladjusted children of divorce. If court battles over custody and visitation must continue, children should enter psychotherapy as a preventive measure to help them gain some psychological distance from their parents' continuing conflict. More important, embattled former spouses should seek counseling for themselves to help them disengage from their angry enmeshment.

Frank hated his former wife, Brenda, and thought she was a terrible mother. Their nine-year-old daughter, Carol, was having behavior problems at school and Frank saw this as further evidence of Brenda's failure as a mother. Carol's fourth-grade teacher described her as one of the "angriest" girls she knew and was concerned because Carol had so little respect for her teachers.

Frank complained to Brenda that she didn't know how to manage Carol properly. He had a long list of things he wanted Brenda to correct in the way she raised both of their daughters, but Brenda was not prepared to listen to his advice. She had divorced Frank to escape from his constant criticisms and efforts to control her, and she was certainly not going to submit to his attempts. Now that she was finally out from under his thumb, Brenda wasn't going to let Frank undermine her independence and confidence again.

Brenda acknowledged that Carol was having real problems at

school, however, and she was having a hard time controlling Carol's behavior at home. But even though she knew something was wrong, Brenda was determined not to let Frank take over and tell her what to do.

As he had several times before, Frank called Brenda to talk about the guidelines he wanted her to follow in raising the girls. Brenda interrupted him before he could finish and said that he could handle Carol his way when she was with him, but that she would do what she thought best when Carol was with her. The argument escalated when Frank claimed that Brenda was obviously an incompetent mother and that "his" daughter was suffering from the consequences of Brenda's inadequacies. If Brenda wouldn't follow his advice, Frank finally said, he would go back to court to gain primary custody of Carol and rise her the "right" way. Brenda shouted one last insult before she angrily hung up the phone.

Five days later, Brenda returned home from work to find two unwanted letters. One, from Frank's attorney, told her that Frank was going to go through with his threat to take her to court. The other letter, which was even more upsetting, was from Carol's teacher, who wanted to discuss the possibility of removing Carol from her class. The teacher's note said that Carol had been a discipline problem all year, but that in the last few days she had become "totally unmanageable."

Neither Brenda nor Frank realized that the continuing conflict between them—not Brenda's mothering—was the source of Carol's school problems. If Brenda and Frank had continued to fight and undermine each other as parents, Carol would probably have remained a behavior problem. In addition, if Frank and Brenda had battled each other in court for control of Carol, Carol would have felt responsible for her parents' conflict and her behavior problems would have escalated. Fortunately, Frank and Brenda's attorneys both supported mediation and they were able to settle this conflict without going back to court. Brenda still found him suffocatingly controlling, and Frank still worried about her parenting competence, but the tension subsided when the court date was dropped. Carol's behavior at school improved almost immediately.

Child Support Disputes

The other issue that brings parents to court and thus increases the likelihood of child adjustment problems is noncompliance with child-support payments. How should a mother respond if the father does not fulfill his financial responsibilities? She should neither protect her former husband by hiding this fact from the children nor use this as a weapon to distance children from him. On the one hand, the financial hardship that results from a father's noncompliance should be honestly presented to children. On the other hand, however, mothers should not refuse visitation privileges as a tactic to obtain money. Although some courts may support mothers who deny contact until support payments are made, this approach often creates further problems for children. Children in this situation are likely to lose whatever relationship they may have had with their father, become harmfully embroiled in parental conflict, and develop significant emotional problems.

A more effective way to secure child-support payments is for the mother to resolve this problem through adult channels and direct confrontation with the father. The first approach is to discuss support payments with the father face-to-face or meet with a neutral mediator to help resolve differences. Most county courts and community mental health agencies have mediation counselors trained to work with these conflicts. Ironically, some delinquent fathers are responding to the feeling that they have no personal relationship with their children. Because their visits with their children are infrequent and dissatisfying, these fathers feel used and resent their financial obligations. Some of these fathers can be brought into financial compliance if the mother guarantees her support for his continuing relationship with the children. Some noncomplying fathers will make child-support payments as soon as they have secured regularly scheduled time with their children.

A different approach is required for fathers who do not want to spend time with their children or contribute to child support. If mediation fails, the mother should then go to court to obtain child-support payments (and request attorney fees for having to go back to court). The family law division of the district attorney's office in your county will prosecute for noncompliance with support payments through wage withholding and property liens.

Previously, courts awarded mothers sole custody of children, long-term alimony, and child-support payments. However, over one-half of all divorced fathers failed to make these payments, and the courts did little to force them to pay. This pattern has been changing since the late 1970s. Courts are now awarding mothers smaller alimony payments and for a shorter period of time because divorced mothers are expected to enter the work force. In contrast, in recent years, courts have become more strict in enforcing child-support payments, and will order wage deductions if fathers do not comply. Thus mothers are more likely to get the legal support they need than they were in the past, but children should not become a bargaining chip in these parental conflicts.

Finances had been the biggest problem for Susan and her three children since the divorce. Although Susan had gone back to work, sold the house, and moved to a low-rent apartment, she still didn't have enough money each month. There was one reason for this: her former husband, Larry, paid less than one-third of the child support that the judge had ordered. Some months he sent nothing, other months he sent part of the payment, but Susan could not remember the last time the full amount had arrived on time. Without his financial help, Susan could not feed, clothe, and shelter a family of four.

The Christmas holidays brought Susan's financial problems to a head. When she realized that her budget could not be stretched to buy even a few modest presents for her children, she knew something had to change. Susan scheduled an appointment with a divorce mediator through the family law division of the county courthouse and told Larry that he could meet her there or in court, whichever he preferred. Larry arrived (ten minutes late) for the first mediation session.

The mediation counselor said she wanted to begin the session by hearing how each of them saw the problem. She asked Susan to begin by telling Larry why she was dissatisfied and what she wanted to change through mediation. In a cool and factual manner, Susan articulated the hardships caused by Larry's failure to make the support payments reliably. The mediator then turned to Larry. "That's how Susan sees the problem, Larry. Will you tell your side of it now?"

Larry exploded. "You never let me have anything to do with the children! You criticized everything I ever did with them. If I tried to change a diaper, you hovered over me giving directions as if I were going to make some fatal mistake. When I tried to feed the baby, you told me I gave her too much food, too fast. When I tried to fix them a sandwich, you'd say I was getting in your way in the kitchen. It seemed as if everytime I was alone with one of the kids you would come in and say something derogatory. You couldn't stand to let me share anything good with them. You always had to be the expert who was in charge of everything. And doing things right meant doing them your way! I finally gave up fighting you for them—you were going to make them *your* children no matter what I did. But you still expect me to pay for it all. What a nice arrangement for you. Go to hell!"

Susan continued to try to explain her good intentions, and Larry continued his angry barrage. The mediator soon regained control of the session, however, and pointed out that angry ventilation was not productive. As the mediator helped both parties become more flexible about their positions and begin to talk more constructively about their children, their tone changed slightly. The session ended with the mediator saying that she thought it was possible to reach a settlement between them and that she was willing to continue meeting with them. Both Larry and Susan agreed to keep meeting and scheduled the next week's appointment.

Susan never agreed with Larry's perception that she kept the children to herself and discouraged his relationship with them. However, she did follow the mediator's suggestion and told Larry that she would sincerely try not to criticize anything he did with the children in the future and that she would actively support and encourage his relationship with them. The mediator also suggested a new visitation plan that gave Larry regularly scheduled time alone with the children. Larry said that it was hard for him to be with all the children at once, and additional arrangements were made for him to see the children one at a time on occasions. In turn, Larry agreed to make the child-support payments each month. Susan accepted this plan, but made it clear that she would file a noncompliance grievance with the family law court and request that his wages be garnished if he did not follow through with regular payment.

Although I have offered suggestions in the preceding pages, no ideal parenting plan will work for every child. Each divorcing couple has to work out arrangements tailored to their child and to their family's needs. The most useful guideline in all custody/visitation arrangements, however, is to balance children's need for a continuing relationship with both parents with children's need to be shielded from ongoing parental conflict. However, in almost all cases, one of the most helpful things parents can do for their children is to keep their personal conflicts with each other from becoming legal battles. Whenever possible, conflicts that arise during and after divorce should be resolved through a neutral mediator. Children will adjust far better when mediation replaces litigation.

PART FOUR

Child-Rearing After Divorce

8

Loyalty Conflicts

Children suffer from loyalty conflicts when they have to choose between their parents. Although divorcing parents need to give children permission to be close to both parents at the same time, in the majority of families, parents give children the message that they must take sides with one parent at the expense of closeness to the other. For example, the mother may subtly communicate that she is hurt or disappointed when her son expresses his eagerness to visit his father. Or the father may overtly say, "Fine, if you want to live with your mother, go. The two of you can have each other as far as I'm concerned." Parents can communicate these loyalty conflicts to their children either directly or covertly. Either way, the result is wrenching for children because being close to one parent means they are being disloyal to the other.

Children want to be close to both parents and will be profoundly distressed if they need to choose one over the other. The stronger the demands for children to take sides and choose, the greater their conflict and the more poorly they adjust to the divorce. Loyalty conflicts always produce adverse symptoms and problems for children, and they are especially likely to occur in families in which children go back and forth between two homes. Parents must reach for a higher standard of ethics and give children overt spoken permission to be as close to the other parent as to themselves.

Loyalty Conflicts Tear Children Apart

I cannot recall one child I have worked with who was having significant, long-term problems adjusting to divorce who was not also struggling with loyalty conflicts. Children are placed in an impossible bind when they feel pressured to take sides or choose between their parents. No child can make this choice without experiencing tremendous inner conflict. Children want a relationship with both parents and will be torn apart inside if they are pulled in two directions by the two parents. As shown by the following case study, the expression "torn apart" captures their experience, as so many of these children complain of headaches and stomachaches.

Although loyalty conflicts can be a problem for children of all ages, nine- to thirteen-year-olds are especially vulnerable to parental pressures to take sides. At these ages, children are especially prone to rigid all-good and all-bad moral judgments. Because they cannot integrate mother's and father's separate version of "the truth," they readily accept implicit parental invitations to choose sides and join one parental camp or the other. When children are pulled into these loyalty conflicts, they usually become insufferably moralistic and judgmental of the other parent.

Understandably, parents want to be assured of their child's loyalty during the crisis of marital separation. An enduring bond of closeness with the children is comforting when ties with the spouse are being torn apart. It is only natural for parents to feel hurt or betrayed by their child's equal interest in the other parent. However, if parents act on these feelings by subtly pressuring children to choose them over the other, children are faced with an unsolvable dilemma. Instead, parents must give children overt spoken permission to love and care for both parents at the same time. When parents can do this, they are truly working in the best interest of their children and they usually will be rewarded with securely adjusted children. The following case is a typical family scenario when loyalty conflicts are occurring.

Mary and Jim had been divorced for eight months. Their middle son, David, developed a very serious symptom during the breakup—a peptic ulcer. Mary called the psychological clinic to request help for the twelve-year-old after their doctor explained that peptic ulcers were a "psychosomatic illness" brought on by emotional tension.

During the initial therapy session with David and his mother, the therapist learned that Mary did not really support David's desire to spend time with his father. Mary described how much she worried when the children were at their father's home. Jim kept guns and ammunition around the house and did not supervise the children as closely as Mary thought was necessary. Mary knew that Jim allowed the children to handle the guns, and she was afraid there would be an accident because of her husband's negligence.

Although the therapist believed that Mary's concern about the guns needed to be taken seriously, she began to wonder whether a broader issue of divided loyalties was being expressed through Mary's anxiety about the guns. The therapist decided to meet together with mother, father, and all three children to see how other family members were reacting to the divorce and to explore her guess about loyalty conflicts.

At the second session, the therapist quickly learned that her hypothesis was correct. As she walked into the treatment room to greet the family, she noted how their seating arrangement reflected the family's alliances. Mother and father sat across the room from each other. The youngest child, the daughter, sat next to her mother, and the older son sat next to his father. In the very center of the room, not one inch closer to mother on the left or father on the right, sat David.

The therapist immediately began to bring the loyalty conflicts out into the open by asking, "What are the teams in this family? Who goes with whom?" Like most families, each family member knew exactly what the teams were. Mother and youngest daughter were together, father and oldest son were allied, and David was precariously in the middle, trying to be on both sides at the same time. Although every family can identify allied teams or subgroups of family members, these alliances are usually much less rigid and exclusive than they were in this family.

The therapist continued to focus on the source of David's loyalty conflicts by asking him, "How does your mother feel when you want to visit your dad?" David replied, "I think she feels bad." The therapist asked, "Do you feel close to your mom and like to spend time with her?" David gave an unusually candid answer for a twelve-year-old by nodding in agreement. The therapist then asked, "How does that make your dad feel?" David again answered with the forthright clarity that children often have about family matters, "I think it makes him mad sometimes."

The therapist's technique of getting David to state his predicament had a strong impact on his parents. If she had suggested to either parent that they were subtly pressuring David to choose, they would have disagreed strongly. However, when they heard David's answers to the therapist, they were dramatically shown how each of them was giving David the message that he should be close to one but not the other. David's conflict over not being free to have a relationship with both of his parents became very evident.

Like most parents, once Jim and Mary saw how the conflict between them was hurting their child, they began to work constructively with the therapist on this problem. In a short time, the parents were able to say to each other that even though they did not like or trust each other, they could see that it was in their children's best interest not to make the children choose between them. They were also able to say to each other in front of the children that they would not make the children choose between them and that they would like the children to have a good relationship with the other parent.

David's ulcer began to improve soon after these conversations. In a few weeks, he was having fewer stomach problems, and at the time of the six-month followup session, his ulcer was virtually cured. Before therapy, David was literally being eaten up inside by the stress of being torn between his parents, both of whom he needed, wanted, and loved. He had been walking on egg shells in his efforts to be close to one while not losing the other. When his parents stopped making David choose between them, the tension causing his ulcer disappeared.

Why Parents Make Their Children Choose

Some parents recognize that their former spouse is just as important to their children as they are. These parents are not threatened by their children's need for the other parent and support their closeness and involvement. At the other extreme are parents who do not wish to acknowledge their children's love for the other parent and demand exclusive loyalty from their children. Most loyalty conflicts fall somewhere in between these two extremes. Many parents who place loyalty conflicts onto children are not fully aware of how they are communicating to their children that being close to the other parent is disappointing or hurtful to them. There are six common reasons why parents may intentionally or unwittingly impose loyalty conflicts on their children.

1. *Anger toward the former spouse.* The most common source of loyalty conflicts for children is parental anger toward the former spouse. As the Greek story of Medea teaches us, the most effective way to retaliate against the other parent is to take their children away. The rage that is often aroused by divorce may seem justified because it is rooted in the feeling of having been exploited and humiliated by the one who left. When this rage is unremitting and continues for many years after the divorce, parents are often using it to defend themselves from their own intolerable feelings of depression, unloveableness, and abandonment, which have been greatly intensified by the breakup. Such parents need to cast the anger and blame, and cling tenaciously to them, in order to deny any responsibility for the marital failure and to bolster their own deeply wounded self-esteem. Unfortunately, some attorneys, therapists, grandparents, and friends fuel this denial and exacerbate long-term adjustment problems for children by supporting the simplistic view that the divorce was perpetrated by an unscrupulous person against a helpless victim.

Traditional sex roles are also the source of much parental anger after divorce. Some mothers demand exclusive loyalty because they are angered by their former husband's new-found interest in the children and shared parenting after the divorce. From their point of view, their husband's lack of parental involvement before the divorce left them abandoned in their child-rearing role. These mothers often feel as if the children are their property, and they may say to themselves, "I'll be damned if I am going to let him take them now. He never had anything to do with them before!" In parallel, of course, these fathers are often angry as well. They counter that their former wives always complained that they didn't do enough for the children, but whenever they tried, their wives resented it and interfered. There is usually some truth to both sides. However, no one can win this argument—only the children lose when parents act on angry feelings by placing loyalty conflicts on children.

2. *Competitiveness between former spouses.* Children caught in

divisive loyalty conflicts often have parents who competed with each other throughout the marriage. And because the greatest area of shared involvement for former spouses is child-rearing, the child's affection or loyalty provides the arena for parents to continue their competition. Fueled by sad and hurt feelings from the breakup, the need to get the better of the former spouse often increases. The irrational belief in this competitive battle is, "If our son cares more about me than he does about you, then it proves I am a better parent." If parents can realize that the child is the only loser in this battle, they may find it easier to back off from their mutual competition. Only then can embroiled former spouses begin to address what they really need to do—disengage from each other emotionally and begin the internal work of psychologically ending the marriage.

3. *Seeking validation.* The child's positive feelings toward the former spouse can arouse unfounded guilt in parents over their decision to divorce. It is painful for parents to see their children feeling sad or longing for the other parent. All too often, parents regard their children's troubled feelings about the divorce as evidence that they should have stayed married. These parents often try to manage their own guilt by trying to dissuade the child from missing or wanting to be with the other parent. The mistaken notion here is: If my child does not want to be with my husband/wife, then my decision to divorce was correct. These parents need to resolve their guilt and accept their children's feelings about the divorce, rather than engendering loyalty conflicts. To illustrate, suppose your child says, "I miss Daddy." Do not invalidate the child's feelings by saying, "But you were just with him over the weekend." Instead, say, "Of course you miss him, and he misses you when he's not with you."

Parents may also engender loyalty conflicts to validate their decision to divorce in a second way. When two people divorce, there is almost always some ambivalence about the breakup. Even though the problems in the relationship ultimately outweigh the rewards, some loving feelings may remain for the ex-spouse. Many parents are afraid of these lingering positive feelings because they fear that continuing to care about or miss their former spouse at times means they should not have divorced. If so, the child's wish to be close to the other parent is threatening because it arouses the parent's own unacceptable positive feelings. Demanding the child's primary loyalty is an ineffective means of protecting oneself from one's own inevitable ambivalence.

Finally, parents may also need their child's favor in order to validate themselves as good parents. Some adults hold the mistaken idea that they are better parents if their child loves them more. It is very gratifying to be the most important person in the whole world to your child. Parents revel in those wonderful but alternating phases of childhood when they are their children's favorite and their children only want them to dress them, bathe them, read to them, or put them to bed. However, when parents' needs for their children's approval becomes too strong, it diminishes their ability to be effective parents. In particular, it is impossible for parents to enforce rules and set limits with their children if they are threatened by their children's disapproval. Parents who need their children's approval can easily be manipulated by their children. Parents need to validate themselves as good parents by doing what they sincerely believe their children need, not what their children want. In other words, parents should focus on doing what is in the child's best interest, not on what will win the child's approval.

4. *Exerting control.* Some parents force their children into loyalty conflicts out of their own need to exert excessive control over their children's lives. Typically, when parents are obsessively controlling, everything must be done their way and they must be in charge of every facet of their children's lives. These parents want the best for their children and believe they know what is best for them. To their continual dismay, however, the children's relationship with the former spouse is one arena that is beyond their control.

Ultimately, one parent cannot determine what the other parent does with the children. For example, some parents strongly disapprove of what the former spouse allows the children to do at his or her home. The rules and routines are usually different at the two households, and these differences are presented to the children as bad or wrong rather than as different. Parents who think in these terms find it hard to accept how their former spouses interact with the children. This disapproval can stem from the insecurity that parents feel when they are not fully in control of the children. Taking the long view, this insecurity is often rooted in insecure attachments during these parents' childhoods, when they tried desperately to exert needed control over their own parents' availability and lack of responsiveness to them.

In order to satisfy this exaggerated need to be in command, parents try to tie the children to them and discourage them from being close to the other parent. Their desire to exercise more control over their children and their former spouse is masked as the "right"way to raise them, and, in fact, these parents are often especially knowledgeable and responsible parents and have legitimate concerns and suggestions. However, it is extremely difficult for these parents to stop criticizing the other parent long enough to consider examining their excessive needs for control. As a result, most parents who repeatedly litigate over the children against their former spouses possess this excessive need for control.

5. *Feelings of loss.* Finally, some parents interpret the child's wish to be with the other parent as another loss for themselves. Many divorcing parents are overly sensitive to even brief periods of separation from their children after the divorce, and very trivial goodbyes can touch on feelings of loss, emptiness, or abandonment. For these parents, the child's desire to be with the other parent may make them feel isolated, as if everyone had left them. In order to protect themselves from painful feelings of rejection and loss, some parents will subtly give their children the message that they have to choose between them and the former spouse. Adults' feelings of loss are an understandable, human response to divorce; however, parents must not avoid these difficult feelings by creating loyalty conflicts for their children.

6. *Separating the child's feelings from the parent's.* Finally, parents also exert loyalty pressures on children because they cannot separate their own negative feelings about the former spouse from their children's need for a continuing and positive relationship with the other parent. Let's consider this very important distinction carefully.

Some parents are able to put aside their differences with their former spouse and support their child's continuing relationship with the other parent. It is not naive to suggest that parents can do this—one third of them do it very well. We don't hear as much about these cooperative parents as we should; they have the most well-adjusted children of divorce. When parents cannot support their children's relationship with the other parent, however, children suffer, especially if one parent criticizes the other parent in order to diminish the child's interest in, affection for, or desire to be with the other parent. When this occurs, one parent is, in effect, trying to remove the other as an object of love for the child.

These combative parents are unable to see their children as separate from themselves—as having feelings and needs that differ from their own. The ability to see children as distinct from oneself—different in their needs and wishes—is an important part of being a good parent. In contrast, it always creates problems for children when one parent is angry and vindictive and wants to undermine children's relationship with the former spouse by shaping their children's feelings to match their own. In effect, these parents are saying to their children, "I cannot accept your wishes, feelings, and needs if they are not the same as mine. If your mother/father is no good for me, she/he is no good for you." This is communicated in parental messages such as, "Your father/mother lied to me for years. You can't trust him/her. You'll see."

This inability to perceive the child's need for a continuing relationship with the other parent as different from the parent's need to end the marital relationship is the source of many problems for children. Thinking this viewpoint is naive, some readers will argue; "If you only knew what my former spouse has done, you'd see why I don't want him/her to have anything to do with the kids." While some people do act destructively and occasionally children need to be removed from such parents for their own protection, in marital counseling, the counselor finds that there are two sides to every story.

For example, an attorney or counselor sits in his office and hears about all the awful things his client's wife has done. He identifies with his client and becomes angry at the man's wife. Somewhere across town, however, that same "awful" wife is telling another attorney or counselor about all the ways she has been injured and abused. That counselor, in turn, identifies with her client. When a mediator or marital counselor sees a couple together, however, it becomes much more difficult to determine who is at fault. Counselors find that there are two different truths in every marriage, each with some legitimacy, and that both spouses contribute, to some degree, to most problems.

Thus, you may hate your former spouse and want nothing more

to do with him or her. That may be the right decision for you, but don't make the same decision for your children. If children consistently spend time with a parent and don't like the way they are responded to, they will want to spend less time with that parent. If children withdraw from the other parent based on their own experience, then this is their choice—but do not make it for them.

Understanding Family Coalitions and Alliances

The loyalty conflicts that children confront after divorce are often exaggerations of alliances, coalitions, or teams that existed in the family before the divorce. The alliances within David's family (the boy with the peptic ulcer in the previous example) are typical. Let's look at this broader issue of family coalitions and alliances more closely.

In healthy, well-functioning families, the primary emotional bond, alliance, or loyalty commitment is between the mother and the father. Both spouses have a primary loyalty to each other and the marital coalition cannot be divided by grandparents, children, friends, employers, or others. Parents will still have differences and conflicts, and they will not exclude or be uncommitted to others, but the marital relationship will be a stable alliance that cannot be disrupted by others. In both intact or divorced families, children adjust better when a primary parental coalition exists because they will not be able to manipulate their parents or play one off against the other. Also, children in such families are free to be close and involved with both parents.

In contrast, in most intact families that have problems with their children, and in almost all marriages that end in divorce, the mother and father have not established a primary alliance that could resist disruption by others. These parents could not establish an effective marital coalition in which their primary emotional needs were met by each other rather than by the children or others, and they could not maintain their own marital relationship as well as a parenting relationship. In addition, these parents could not address and resolve their conflicts; rather, they avoided conflict or routinely embroiled a third person in their marital conflicts to divert them from the issues that they needed to address. When parents cannot establish an effective marital coalition with each other, they usually form their primary emotional bond with one or more of their children. In this situation, one spouse becomes an outsider to this parent–child coalition and generally resents the exclusion. Problems arise for children in such a family constellation because they feel guilty and disloyal to the primary parent if they want to be close to the outside parent as well.

The best way to learn more about family alliances is to draw a map of the patterns of relationships that existed in your family before the divorce. Take a pen or pencil now and begin to draw a three-generational map that includes all the members of your family before the divorce: paternal and maternal grandparents, parents, and children (see Figure 8.1). The question to answer here is "Who goes with whom?" Based on the bonds of emotional closeness and involvement, what is the primary two-person relationship in the family? Is it between mother and father, or is there some other primary pairing, such as mother and daughter? What other two-person coalitions or alliances exist—for example, grandparent and parent, child and child? Can larger subgroups with three or more members be identified? Circle the members of each of these subgroups. Who is on the outside of this larger group? Is there an outsider who does not belong to any subgroup? Do all the children side with one parent and not the other?

In figure 8.1, the mother and father do not form the primary couple relationship in the family; it is formed instead by the mother and oldest daughter. The oldest daughter, the mother, and the maternal grandmother also form a subgroup in the family. Therefore, if the oldest daughter wants more of a relationship with her father

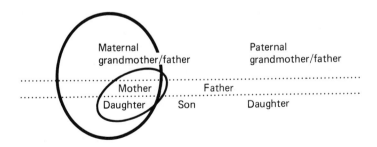

FIGURE 8–1

A Three-Generational Map

after the divorce, she may feel guilty for breaking her longstanding alliance with her mother by approaching her father. This daughter may feel that she must sacrifice her relationship with her father in order to remain loyal to her mother. She is far more likely to develop symptoms and problems after the divorce than her younger brother and sister,who are freer to be involved with both their mother and their father.

It is also common in some families for all of the children to be allied with their mother, while the father is the outsider. These children usually feel guilty and awkward if they try to develop more of a relationship with their father after the divorce. But, whatever the family constellation, children need to be as close as possible to both of their parents, and so divorcing parents need to be aware of cross-generational alliances that foster competing coalitions and exclusive loyalty ties for their children. The problems in structural family relationships that originally contributed to the divorce must be acknowledged or they may continue to cause problems after the divorce.

An Agreement for Parental Cooperation

It is often very difficult for angry former spouses to support each other as parents. Even otherwise loving and responsible parents routinely disrupt the child's relationship with the other parent by undermining the other's parenting authority or pressuring children to take sides. Parents vent their feelings of injustice to the children, for example, by saying, "Your father is leaving *us* for another woman!" or "You have to change schools and move because your mother is so selfish that she cares more about herself than she does about our family." Although hurt and angry feelings are understandable, parents must remember that their children suffer when their relationship with the other parent is compromised. Reaching for the best part of themselves, parents should encourage children to have the best relationship they possibly can with the other parent. As hard as this can be to do, it is the most loving gift divorcing parents can give to their children.

To help parents cooperate together, sample scripts to help divorcing parents communicate their intentions and a parental contract for them to sign are provided in this section. These scripts and the contract emphasize three points: (1) each parent must support the other's parental role and not undermine the former spouse's authority with the children; (2) parents must not expose children to parental fighting or embroil them in parental conflicts; and (3) parents must not make children choose between them, but should encourage them to be close to both parents at the same time. I suggest that divorcing parents sit down together and discuss the scripts and the contract that follow. After modifying or rewriting them to fit your circumstances, agree to follow these guidelines as closely as possible.

1. Each of you must support the other's role as parent. You cannot undermine each other by saying such things as: "You don't have to pay attention to your father, he only sees you on weekends. I'm the one who is really raising you" or "Your mother's crazy. Come to me if you have any problems with her." Rather, make the following commitment by speaking it aloud to each other:

> I will support you in your role as [child's name] parent. You have an important part in deciding how [she/he] is raised. I will not make fun of you or disparage you to our child. I will encourage [him/her] to respect and care about you.

2. You must also encourage your child to have a close and loving relationship with the other parent. Many times parents give off cues, verbal or nonverbal, that make the child feel obliged to choose between the two of you. Make the following commitment by saying aloud to each other:

> I will encourage [child's name] to be with you and talk about you without making [him/her] feel disloyal to me. I will encourage [child's name] to have a close and loving relationship with both of us at the same time. I will not pressure our child to choose me over you.

3. The problems that arise between the two of you must be settled without involving your children in any way. Avoid sending messages to each other through the child, such as "Tell your mother to stop calling me at work" or "Tell your father he'd better not be

late with the support check again." Make a commitment by saying aloud to each other:

> I will not use our child when I am angry with you, but will try to deal with you directly instead. When there are conflicts between us, you and I can discuss them together and decide what is in our child's best interest.

Each parent should sign an agreement of intent:

> I agree to try to support [spouse's name]'s parental relationship with our children. I will not try to undermine that relationship with our children, make the children choose between us, or involve the children in our disagreements. Although I probably will not be able to do this all of the time, I realize that this is in the best interest of our children and I will try to follow these guidelines as best I can.
>
> Signed

The preceding scripts and the contract lay down the ground rules parents must try to follow to support their children's development. In addition, parents must actively enlist grandparents, teachers, and other significant adults to take a neutral stance toward the divorce. Children need grandparents, family friends, and teachers to be supportive without taking sides or blaming either parent. Other adults should be informed that they are more helpful if they respond to complaints from one parent about the former spouse by making positive rather than critical comments—for example, "It sounds like the divorce is being hard on everybody in your family.

Children cannot attain a secure identity if grandparents, teachers, and others express their love for one parent by criticizing the other. All of the adults in and around the family must not further polarize parents; instead, they should encourage children to have a close and continuing relationship with both parents. Every child is half mother and half father, and children adjust better when they have permission to be close to both parents at the same time.

9

Parentification: Turning Children into Adults

In healthy families, adults nurture and guide and children receive and follow. Single-parent families that function well have clearly defined intergenerational boundaries that separate adult business from child business. By necessity, children in single-parent families usually need to take on more household duties, and there is often more emotional sharing between parent and child than in two-parent families. Thus, children in single-parent families grow up faster, and they have to do more chores and make more decisions for the family. Even so, however, roles and responsibilities are clearly differentiated between adults and children in healthy single-parent families. The single parent still performs the leadership functions for the family, such as providing a well-organized household with predictable daily routines, making decisions and plans for the family, and setting limits and enforcing rules for children. Furthermore, although parents have legitimate needs for companionship and support, these needs are met primarily in same-generational peer relationships rather than through the children.

This fundamental model for family life often goes awry in the aftermath of divorce. Some single-parent families have problems when adult and child roles are not clearly distinguished, when boundaries between the adult and the child generations are blurred, and when adults have too many personal needs met through the children. In these families, children take over so many adult responsibilities, or try to meet so many of their parents' emotional needs, that the roles of parent and child become reversed. Family therapists call this role reversal *parentification*.

Most parents are not familiar with the concept of parentification, and the idea is easily misunderstood at first. This role reversal occurs in several different ways. Children are parentified when they take over so many household responsibilities that they in effect become the parent in the family. These responsibilities may include babysitting, cleaning, fixing dinner, disciplining younger children, and other tasks. More subtly, but more commonly, this switching of roles also occurs when children assume a disproportionate sense of responsibility for a parent's emotional well-being. These children take care of the parent at the expense of their own needs.

What is the difference between a child who is put in the position of acting like a parent and a child who is simply asked to be appropriately responsible and helpful? The distinction is a question of degree. In talking about parentification, I am not suggesting that children should be spoiled or raised to be unresponsive to parental needs and concerns. It is important for children to share in household duties and to learn that they can give to parents as well as receive from them. Parentification occurs when a line is crossed and too many of the adult's needs and responsibilities are being met by the child. These children who are turned into pseudoadults and confidants are often described as perfect, but they suffer adverse consequences in the long run.

Three Types of Parentification

Parentification usually occurs in one of three ways: when children provide security and controls for their parent; when they meet parents' needs for intimacy and closeness; or when they run the household and become the primary caregiver for younger siblings. Each of these three styles of parentification merits a closer examination.

Providing Security

In response to the stress of divorce and the increased demands of being a single parent, some parents begin to meet too many of their adult needs through their children. When a boy is parentified and given an adult role in the family, he is often encouraged to provide stability, guidance, or control for his parent. In this particular form of role reversal, boys are called on to take care of the adult. In our first example, a very adult little boy has learned to take care of his mother extremely well, even though he is only nine years old. Although this competence and caring seems very positive at first glance, on further inspection we can see that it is highly **problematic**. Let's look at one experience that is typical of how this boy took care of his mother, rather than having her take care of him.

Jeff's parents had recently divorced and he was moving with his mother and two younger sisters to a new city. Jeff was sitting next to his mother in the front seat of the car and his two sisters were in the back. As they approached the new city, Jeff's mother began to feel overwhelmed by the prospect of resettling her family and beginning a new life on her own.

Little Jeff had already learned to be highly attentive and responsive to his mother's concerns. He sensed her anxiety as soon as it began and he reassured her that everything would work out all right. Jeff told his mom that she was a good mother and that she would be able to find a job soon. Yet, despite his reassurances and sympathy, Jeff's mother still felt upset and had difficulty finding the right exits from the busy freeway. Without being asked, Jeff reached into the glove compartment for a map and started locating the exits they needed. At only nine years of age, Jeff was reading a road map and showing his mother where she should go.

What is the meaning of this brief scenario? Jeff is providing too much control and direction for his mother. He is acting as a parent and taking care of his mother, rather than behaving like the child he is and being taken care of by his mother.

It is remarkable that Jeff can read a map at such a young age—he has skills that many teenagers don't possess. Like most boys who have been forced into adult roles, Jeff has not only learned to be competent and effective, he is also sensitive and reassuring to his mother. What is wrong with raising such a competent and helpful son? Isn't it desirable for a child to be supportive during a time of stress? Of course, it is, but only if this type of adult behavior happens only occasionally.

If the mother later regains her composure and takes on the role of parent, the result will be able, perceptive children who have learned that they can give as well as receive. However, when this way of responding characterizes the parent–child relationship, as it did for Jeff, the child is acting as a parent to the adult. Although children like Jeff get along very well throughout childhood, they will begin to feel the troublesome consequences of switching roles when they reach late adolescence and early adulthood.

Providing Intimacy and Closeness

When a marriage ends, adults usually lose whatever intimacy or affection they may have shared with their spouse. The second type of parentification occurs when parents begin to meet these needs for closeness through their children. Parents who describe their children as their "best friend" or their "lifeline" or who characterize their relationship as having "a very special kind of closeness" are usually meeting emotional needs through their children that should be met through relationships with other adults.

These valid human needs for closeness are quite appropriate; however, it is essential that parents meet these needs for personal sharing and support through other adults rather than through their children. Meeting adult needs for intimacy and friendship through children is the form of parentification that is most likely to occur with daughters. In the example below, we can see how exciting and rewarding it is for a girl to be put in the adult role of mother's friend and confidante.

Even before the divorce Mrs. Winter had always been especially close to her ten-year-old daughter, Joan. Mrs. Winter and her mother had shared a special kind of closeness that had been very important to both of them, and she now enjoyed that same kind of closeness with her daughter. Mrs. Winter began to describe her daughter as her "best friend" and praised Joan for being so reliable since the divorce.

Joan liked this close relationship with her mother. Although she wished her parents had not divorced, things were better now. Joan missed seeing her father sometimes, but they had never been very close. Joan knew she was even more important to her mother than ever, so seeing less of her father was a trade-off she could live with.

Joan and her mother talked over all the significant things in Mrs.

Winter's life. Joan knew that her mother was mad at a friend for gossiping about her at work, and she even knew all of the untrue things this friend had said. Joan also listened to her mother's worries about money, and knew that they only had $24,000 a year to live on now, compared to $55,000 before the divorce.

The most confidence they shared was what went on during her mother's dates. Mrs. Winter would describe the men she went out with and regularly asked Joan whether she should keep dating them. Mrs. Winters also confided to her daughter whether her date had tried to kiss her before she felt she knew him well enough, and soon Joan was asking her mother's boyfriends where they would be going, what they would be doing, and when they would be home. Mrs. Winter would laugh, delighted at Joan's concern, but Joan worried about her mother when her mother was out. Joan would sit, anxiously awaiting her return, and then they would laugh and giggle as they discussed her mother's love life late into the night. Joan felt so grown-up and important because she could talk with her mother about such adult concerns. In fact, her girlfriends at school had begun to sound silly and childish in comparison.

Running the Household

The third type of parentification can occur with children as young as six or seven years, but usually happens to older teenaged boys and girls. These children are given parental responsibilities for rearing younger siblings and managing the home. In the previous two examples, children met parents' emotional needs, which should have been met by other adults, by acting as adults and taking care of their parents. In this third form of role reversal, children are not required to fulfill emotional needs, but instead are asked to take over adult responsibilities and duties for childcare and running the household when a parent has abdicated.

Boys and girls who are asked to provide security and intimacy do not resist these attempts; in fact, they readily take this role and are reluctant to relinquish it. It is highly rewarding for children to have such a powerful and important role in relation to their parents. However, by contrast, adolescents who are forced to take over child-rearing and homemaking responsibilities often become angry and rebellious, and young children usually become depressed and compliant. For instance, many oldest daughters in single-parent families take on the role of mother and feed, dress, and discipline their younger siblings every day. When this kind of parentification occurs, the adolescent is not just taking on her fair share of the family workload, she is taking over and fulfilling the parent's child-rearing obligations. Many fourteen- to eighteen-year-old girls become pregnant and marry in order to get out of the family and escape this type of parentification. The following example shows how fifteen-year-old Mike angrily rebels against his parentified role.

Mike and his divorced mother, Nancy, had been at war for well over a year—ever since Mike's father had been transferred overseas. When her former husband moved away, the entire responsibility for raising their three children fell to Nancy. The children's father used to take them to his house on many weekends, and they would often go away on trips with him when they had vacations from school. This relief from the demands of raising three children while working and trying to go to school part-time had been a lifesaver for Nancy.

Once this respite was taken away, however, Nancy began to feel smothered by the constant demands of raising her three children. To cope with the mounting resentment and depression, Nancy began to give fifteen-year-old Mike increased responsibility for taking care of her seven-year-old daughter and ten-year-old son.

Within six months of his father's departure, Mike was running the household almost entirely by himself. Nancy expected Mike to come home and take care of his little sister after school and to start dinner. Two nights a week, when Nancy went directly from work to evening classes, Mike was expected to fix dinner, clean up, and put the younger children to bed before Nancy returned at 10:00 P.M. Nancy also wanted some time to herself on weekends and asked Mike to babysit with his brother and sister because Nancy could not afford to hire a babysitter. Nancy felt guilty about giving so many responsibilities to Mike, however, because she felt as if she were a bad mother. Her guilt only made her want to stay away from home even more.

The seven-year-old daughter, Laura, was sad about her father's departure, and now she felt that her mother was leaving her, too.

She began to whine and plead for her mother to stay home more, so that Nancy felt even more guilty and more like escaping from the home. The younger brother, Doug, resented the fact that Mike could tell him what to do all the time. As Doug became angrier, it was harder for Mike or Nancy to discipline him. Soon the two boys were fighting constantly.

Mike was angry at everyone. He hated his mother for putting so many demands on him, and he turned this hostility toward Laura and Doug. But at the same time that he resented this parental role, it also felt good to be in charge. Mike liked having so much power in the family and he did not want to give up his authority when Nancy returned home. Nancy and Mike began quarreling like a married couple over who was in charge. Chaos soon developed because no one was in effective control of the family. At this point Nancy called the psychological clinic and asked for help with her "uncontrollable" teenage son.

The Adverse Consequences of Parentifying Children

Why is parentification such a big problem for children? What are the negative consequences for children such as Jeff, Joan, or Mike? To understand the problems that follow from parentification we need to look at both the short-term and the long-term effects. The problems of parentification usually are not evident in childhood; instead, they appear during the transition from late adolescence to early adulthood. Rather than exhibiting symptoms and problems, children like Jeff and Joan are exceptionally well-behaved and too often described as perfect. They are pleasant children for adults to be around because they are more mature and responsible than other children their own age. Instead of making demands on their parents, as normal children do, these children satisfy parental needs and make adults feel better. This type of parentification can easily occur because this subtle role reversal is gratifying for both the parent and the child in the short run. Adults have their needs taken care of and the child enjoys the power and importance of this special adult role.

However, it is always harmful when children become responsible for, or take care of, the emotional needs of their parents. The natural flow of nurturing from parent to child is reversed, and the child's age-appropriate dependency needs are not met. Although parentified children initially enjoy this relationship with their parents, as adults they come to resent having been used by their parent and having been deprived of their own childhoods.

The long-term effects of having been parentified are significant. Parentified children grow up to feel overly responsible for others, afraid of depending on others, and guilty about having their own needs met. Because the basic model of relationships they have learned is taking care of others, parentified children often re-enact the roles of provider or rescuer in subsequent relationships. For example, they often select careers as nurses, ministers, teachers, or counselors. Although kind and capable, they feel guilty about saying no, setting limits, and meeting their own legitimate needs. Because they do not draw boundaries well, they tend to overidentify with others' problems and are prone to burnout. Since they grew up having to take care of their parents, they feel threatened by relinquishing this control in their adult lives. For example, it may be hard for them to share work-related responsibilities, although at the same time they resent having to "do everything." These control issues may surface as symptoms such as airplane phobias, for example, when they must temporarily relinquish control to the pilot. These parentified children also have problems in their personal lives because to be intimate with someone they must take the threatening step of relinquishing control.

Thus, serious consequences result from this role reversal. These problems become evident when the parentified child grows older and tries to become a mature adult. The paradox is that children who have acted as adults throughout their childhoods have difficulty becoming adults. With this in mind, let's focus on the developmental process of leaving home during late adolescence and becoming an independent adult.

Emancipation from the Family

During late adolescence and early adulthood, young people pass through a developmental stage of emancipation from the family. At this point, young people physically and psychologically leave their family of origin and become independent adults ready to begin their own families. This process of emancipation involves three complex activities.

First, young adults move away from home and establish their own separate residence at college, in the service, or in an apartment with friends. At this stage, the importance of the young adults' relationship with their parents should shrink compared to those with friends and lovers. Second, translating interests and abilities into career goals and success also becomes an important part of establishing an adult identity that is independent of the parents. Finally, young adults must explore religious and political alternatives as a means of clarifying their own values and personal beliefs.

The problem with role reversal is that parentified children may not be able to psychologically leave their parents and successfully negotiate these three developmental hurdles. It is difficult for such children to establish their own independent adult lives as they should at this age.

Because parentified children have grown up feeling responsible for their parent, it is difficult for them to leave home, both psychologically and physically. This transition is especially difficult for girls. Daughters feel that their mothers still need them, will be lonely without them, or cannot cope alone. Joan, from the example, will feel guilty when she leaves her mother to establish her own home, pursue a career, and marry. The special closeness she has experienced with her mother is also a binding closeness that will prevent Joan from feeling good about herself as a competent and independent adult away from her mother.

Parentified children such as Joan also have difficulty succeeding as adults because they still feel that they must respond to their parents' wishes and needs, rather than defining and carrying out their own plans and dreams. As a young adult, Joan will feel torn by this conflict in several ways. She will be prone to feeling guilty, depressed, and selfish whenever she becomes stronger, more successful, or gets what she wants. Joan may remain unsure about her career plans for many years and become anxious or depressed, rather than happy and proud, whenever she succeeds. In particular, it is likely that Joan will have trouble establishing a love relationship with a man who can respond to her needs. She will be caught in a bind because she will feel she must always give; she has never learned to receive or be taken care of. Finally, Joan will probably feel guilty about betraying her mother and forsaking her for another relationship.

Children who have been used as pseudoadults also find it difficult to establish intimate relationships in young adulthood, especially boys, such as Jeff, who have taken care of a parent rather than being taken care of. As a result of this role reversal, appropriate childhood dependency needs have not been met, and as adults they will be threatened by having their legitimate needs for affection and caring fulfilled. Because taking affection is so unfamiliar to them, these children don't know how to respond. As an adult, loving involves giving and receiving equally, and in order to receive love as an adult, you must have been comfortable doing so as a child. Parentified children also have trouble with intimacy because they are afraid of relinquishing their power and control, even temporarily. Furthermore, getting close to another may trigger the fear of once again having to take over and be responsible for this person, just as these children did with their parent while growing up.

Thus, for parentified children, natural needs to be cared for or valued by others seem like a pit of shameful dependency that was never satisfied in childhood. In order to avoid conflicts around their own needs, children who switched roles with their parent will often establish love relationships with needy, problem-ridden partners whom they can "rescue." Or they may avoid intimacy and commitment through promiscuity. Either way, it will be hard for a boy like Jeff to have a mutually responsive love relationship with a woman.

In addition, parentified children often cannot gain a realistic sense of their own power and control. When children must take on adult roles, they become too important to the parent and exert too much influence over the parent's well-being. As a result, these children often gain an exaggerated sense of their own importance and of their ability to influence others. Children cannot gain a realistic sense of their own limits and capabilities when they are encouraged in the illusion that they can prop up a parent's sagging self-esteem, maintain their parents' emotional equilibrium, or make important decisions for their parents.

On the other side of their grandiosity, however, these parentified children have a parallel sense of their own inadequacy. This feeling of inadequacy, which is often a constant source of anxiety, arises because they never were capable of meeting their parents' needs. It is only an illusion that the child can fulfill the parent's emotional needs. As a result of this family myth, parentified children often suffer from strong performance anxieties as adults and feel inadequate to meet the exaggerated demands they place on themselves.

Finally, children who have spent their youths acting as parents have other problems as young adults. Jeff, Joan, and Mike have all lost their chance to be a child, and they will often experience an inner emptiness. For example, parentified children may reflect this emptiness by saying, "I feel as if there is a hole inside me." This emptiness occurs because the natural flow of parental care to a dependent child has not occurred and these children have not "taken in."

Why Parentification Occurs

Stages of the Family Life Cycle

Many parents see their divorce as an isolated experience that just happened or came by surprise. However, if we expand this perspective and look at the psychological issues that couples must resolve at different stages of the family life cycle, parents can better understand the divorce and why parentification, loyalty conflicts, and other problems occur. To gain this understanding, we must leave divorce temporarily and examine some broader issues of family development.

BECOMING A COUPLE. The birth of the family is during the couple's courtship and engagement period. Many of the difficulties that parents have during marriage and even following divorce are problems that were never satisfactorily resolved in this first stage. Family researchers have identified a number of psychological tasks that the new couple must complete in order to have a successful marriage. For example, the couple must establish mutually satisfying routines for making decisions and resolving differences between them: How will they manage money? When will they make love? How will they divide work and other household responsibilities? Will the couple spend their leisure time alone, visiting family, or developing contacts with business associates? Under what circumstances does the husband, or the wife, make these decisions? Couples do not sit down and overtly devise rules for doing all of these things, but every couple must gradually evolve stable and mutually satisfying patterns for their life together. If the partners do not talk together about their preferences, or if one is not responsive to the other's wishes, the groundwork is laid for future problems.

The most important task during this stage of becoming a couple is for both partners to shift their primary loyalty and commitment from their parents to each other. As observed in chapter 8, the couple must establish a primary coalition in which the spouse comes first, and parents, friends, and work come second. Chronic marital conflict results when one or both partners retain primary allegiance or loyalty to parents instead of to their new spouse.

The familiar ritual of the wedding ceremony enacts the concepts of shifting loyalty from the family of origin to the spouse and forming a primary marital coalition. A central purpose of the ceremony is to publicly mark the transition in loyalty from the parents and family of origin to the new spouse as family, friends, and clergy assemble for the ceremony and the father walks the bride to the front of the church. In front of all, the father symbolically gives the bride away by placing her hand in the hand of the waiting groom, stepping back from the couple, and sitting down beside his wife. The bride and groom, now separated from the parental generation, turn away and step forward to be married and to publicly announce themselves to family and friends as an enduring marital couple.

Shifting loyalty bonds from parents to the new spouse is a major developmental task. This transition is difficult for most families, but it is especially troublesome in families without a primary marital coalition. The question of who comes first, parent or spouse, may be painfully enacted in conflicts over planning the wedding. For example, young adults who are still embroiled in cross-generational alliances often face a wrenching battle over whether the ceremony should be conducted the way the couple wants it done or the parents' way. The underlying conflict concerns shifting loyalties from the previous generation to the spouse, but it is played out in arguments over who will be invited to the wedding, where it will be held, how it will be conducted, who is financially responsible, and so forth. In contrast, couples who enjoy their wedding day often have been able to switch their primary loyalty from their parents to each other. Such couples are not being pulled apart by guilt-inducing, competing loyalty ties.

Thus, couples who have successfully formed a marital bond by shifting their primary loyalties from parents to spouse are able to maintain a united front that cannot be divided by parents or others. If they have not established this primary marital coalition, couples will have more difficulty in the next stage of family formation—having children.

BECOMING A PARENT. Ideally, the newlyweds will have a few years together to consolidate their relationship before the birth of the first child. This change from a two-person to a three-member family is challenging and demanding. Most couples do not anticipate how much the new baby will alter their one-to-one adult relationship or how much time and attention the baby will require. Successful couples need to keep their marital bond intact by spending time together as a couple and maintaining their private psychological closeness. Unless the marital relationship is continually nurtured and given its fair share of attention, it will suffer in the busy months that follow birth. Thus, the major psychological task for the couple at this stage is to meet the many demands of parenting but, at the same time, maintain their personal relationship.

Many couples fail in this task and the marital relationship is lost as a result, especially if they have not completed the previous stage's psychological business of establishing a primary marital coalition. Such couples do not continue to go out or spend time alone together, and responding to their children's needs always seems to take precedence over their relationship. Over time, one parent may resent the child or the spouse and feel unimportant, as if the child is the only one who matters to the spouse. Couples who lose their marital relationship to the parental role are more likely to divorce and to continue this conflict afterward.

As noted in chapter 8, loyalty conflicts are especially likely to occur when the couple never established a primary marital coalition during the initial stage of couple formation. As a result, inappropriate cross-generational alliances develop between parent and child to fill the void. Cross-generational alliances created before the breakup are usually exacerbated by shared parenting arrangements after divorce, as parents further pressure children to take sides in parental battles.

Similarly, parentification can also result when psychological requirements of family formation have not been met. When newlyweds have not psychologically separated from their families of origin or have not communicated well enough to resolve the basic tasks of becoming a couple, they will not be able to form a primary marital coalition. With the birth of the first child in the next stage of family life, they will not be able to cooperate and communicate effectively enough to meet the demands of the new baby while still preserving their marital relationship. In this situation, the mother usually turns to the child (and simultaneously to her own mother) to get basic relationship needs met while the father distances himself from both the mother and the children.

Several years later, the lack of a marital coalition and increasing emotional distance often lead to divorce when children reach preschool and school age. The already distant father usually becomes even more uninvolved after the divorce, and the alliance between the mother and the child leads to even more dependency and inappropriate closeness between them. As the mother tries to cope with the stresses of divorce and raising children on her own, intergenerational boundaries and the distinction between the roles of parent and child become even more blurred. Parentification usually begins at this point, as parents begin to have too many of their own personal needs for support, affection, or companionship met through their children. Because it may be difficult for single parents to determine objectively whether parentification is occurring, some specific guidelines for assessing this are offered in the following section.

Assessing Parentification in Your Family

The urge to rely on a child for comfort is great as parents try to cope with the stresses of divorce and single-parenting. It's fine for children to serve occasionally as listening posts, but the family becomes dysfunctional if this practice becomes habitual. Parents must not consistently rely on support from sons or daughters and must not treat them as peers. Even though children love their parents deeply and want to help, they are not equals and are not equipped for adult problems and needs. As we have seen, if children feel that they are the glue holding the family together, they will have a difficult time leaving home and successfully starting a life of their own. By answering the following questions, parents can determine for themselves whether they are parentifying their children.

1. Do your children know that you are in charge of the family? Even though single parents need more help from their children, successful single parents communicate clearly that they are the adults and that they are in charge. It benefits everyone if your children feel they have important jobs and responsibilities that help contribute to the family. However, if your reliance on your children interferes with their schoolwork or their time to play with friends, it's too much.

2. Do you put your child in the role of confidant or emotional caretaker? You are more likely to do this if you do not have adult friends with whom you can share your problems. Single parents have enormous responsibilities, workloads, and stress, and they need friends and confidants. However, these legitimate needs must be met by other adults, not by your children. Support groups for parents, such as Parents Without Partners, are available in most communities.

3. Do your children regularly see you crying, feeling helpless, and getting upset when things go wrong? Do you discuss financial problems and worries with them? Most people underestimate how much children worry about their parents and how ready they are to take care of their parent's distress. It promotes growth when children are aware of their parents' concerns, but awareness becomes worry when children see emotional outbursts. Similarly, close becomes too close when children are pulled into financial anxieties that take them away from their appropriate childhood concerns about school and peers. Establish a buddy system with another single parent so that you don't need to unburden yourself on your children.

4. Do you discuss your dating relationships with your child? Dating relationships are for adults, not children, and parents should not involve children in this aspect of their personal lives. Single parents should also keep dates and children separate until it seems certain that the relationship will continue for a long time. Your sex life is adult business and private; children and adolescents should not be informed.

5. Do you use your child as a buffer or intermediary between you

and others? If you ask your child to carry messages to your former spouse, or to spy and report on what the former spouse is doing, you are placing your children in an adult role and asking them to meet your needs at their expense. Similarly, if you make your children answer the telephone or door and filter unwanted callers for you, you may be parentifying your child. The adult should be the gatekeeper between the family and others; don't put children between you and others who are difficult for you to deal with. Although this may sound trivial, putting the adult's voice on the telephone answering machine may be one good way to announce to everyone that the parent is leading this family, not the child.

6. Do you describe your child as your best friend or your lifeline, or do you or others characterize your child as perfect? Although it is extremely gratifying to be very close to such a well-behaved child, it is a bad sign. "Perfect" children are often too anxious and worried about their parents to act like children. Similarly, it's very stimulating for children to be a special friend to their parent, but it also burdens them with responsibility for their parent's well-being. Parents in this situation should actively focus children away from concerns about the parent and toward childhood involvements. Some parents may want to tell their children that they should only have three jobs to worry about: doing well in school, making good friendships that last, and doing at least one enjoyable thing every day.

With only one parent in the family, the boundary line between adult responsibilities and the children's inevitably becomes less distinct because the single parent must rely on the children far more than in two-parent families. If this reliance is not overdone, the increased demands for support can produce healthy children who are empathic and capable. However, a distinction between the roles of parent and child must be maintained for the family to function effectively. If this line has been crossed, adults need to reclaim the role of guide, leader, and nurturer. Children adjust far better when parents take charge and the children follow.

10

Child-Rearing Practices

Although parents intended to change only the husband-wife relationship through divorce, they soon learn that their relationships with their children have altered as well. In particular, the daily business of raising children is usually very different following divorce. Unfortunately, researchers have found that parents' ability to discipline and nurture their children and to provide an organized household routine and structure often declines after divorce. When this occurs children are more likely to develop emotional and behavioral problems, and parents need to consider which child-rearing practices will most effectively foster their children's successful adjustment after the divorce.

Three Approaches to Discipline

Parents discipline their children in one of three ways. Most use either an authoritarian approach that is strict but harsh, or a permissive approach that is loving but lax. Neither practice works as well as the lesser-known authoritative approach, which combines firm limits with affection and stresses communication and explanations for rules. Although most parents believe they must be either strict or loving, the authoritative parent can be both at the same time. Let's look at these three styles of discipline more closely.

Authoritarian Parenting

Perhaps the most common (and ineffective) method of discipline is the authoritarian approach. Authoritarian parents give children clear expectations for what behavior is acceptable and unacceptable. Parental rules are clearly explained and the consequences for violating them are consistently enforced. Authoritarian parents also have high expectations that their children will behave in a responsible and mature manner. Children are expected to perform up to the limits of their abilities and to be competent and contributing family members.

However, authoritarian parents do not give their children reasons or explanations for their demands. The child is expected to obey without questioning or trying to understand why the parent has set these limits. Children cannot ask why a rule is set—they must simply obey. For example, children who grow up in an authoritarian household regularly hear their parents make statements such as: "Don't ever ask me *why* you can't go out. I am your father. You'll do what I say, or else!" Furthermore, there is no room for compromise or verbal give-and-take between the parent's and the child's wishes. Children are not encouraged to suggest alternatives or to explain their side of the story. Most importantly, however, authoritarian parents do not couple their stern directives with much warmth or affection. Children usually experience such parents as cold, distant, and intimidating.

The threat of parental power and the fear of rejection do keep children in line, especially while they are young. Although this approach is certainly better for children than having no discipline at all, it does have major drawbacks. Children obey, but do so out of fear. As a result, the insecurity children feel with their parent often generalizes into a fear of teachers, coaches, principals, and other adults in their lives. While some children remain afraid of their authoritarian parents, others become rebellious and defiant as they grow older, stronger, and more verbal.

Another drawback to the authoritarian approach is that it limits the growth of children's intellectual abilities. When children are not given reasons to help them understand why parents have set certain rules and are not encouraged to suggest alternatives or compromises, they do not learn to exercise language and reasoning skills. Children of authoritarian parents score lower on verbal tests of intelligence than children who are given an opportunity to interact with parents over rules and directives.

In healthy development, children learn to obey, but without sacrificing their own initiative and positive self-image. Healthy children become self-controlled and self-reliant without losing their sense of being prized by their parents. For children of authoritarian parents, however, the trade-off between acting on their own wishes and maintaining parental approval is too severe. Because authoritarian parents provide too little nurturance and affection, too much of their children's initiative and positive self-regard is forsaken in order to secure parental approval. These children are obedient, but they are also anxious and insecure because they comply with parents out of fear. These well-behaved, insecure children become harsh, critical, and demanding toward themselves, just as their parents have been toward them. As adults, many children from highly authoritarian families struggle with excessive guilt, depression, unassertiveness, anxiety, and low self-esteem. These neurotic feelings and conflicts will usually be present even though these people are responsible, hard-working, and successful adults.

Permissive Parenting

The authoritarian parent correctly recognizes that children need to know the rules and that they will be enforced; however, authoritarian discipline is harsh and uncompromising. In contrast, other parents may err on the side of permissiveness. Although permissive parents provide more affection than authoritarian parents, they are not able to take a firm stance and place appropriate controls on the children's behavior.

Permissive parents are lax disciplinarians. Their children do not know what behavior is expected of them and they do not know what will happen if they violate parental norms. Most importantly, permissive parents do not consistently enforce the few rules they set. As a result, children of permissive parents learn that they do not have to obey because parents will not enforce the rules. Thus permissive parents are often expressive, loving, and communicative, but their children are not disciplined and are not expected to behave in a mature, responsible manner. Without parental expectations that they perform to the best of their abilities, children do not develop the skills and capabilities to succeed on their own.

The children of permissive parents also have adjustment problems later in life. These indulged children are more likely to develop behavior problems. For example, they are more likely to get into trouble with school authorities for truancy, to be picked up by the police for reckless driving, or to become involved with drugs and alcohol. Finally, as adults, they tend to be more self-centered, demanding, and exploitative in their interpersonal relations and less capable of making commitments and following through on obligations.

Why do these problems develop? Children of permissive parents often learn that they can avoid the consequences of their own behavior. Rules and limits do not necessarily apply to them, and their wishes can often be gratified without delay. Researchers have found these children to be dependent, immature, demanding, and unhappy. They have little self-control, low tolerances for frustration, and get along poorly with their peers.

Authoritative Parenting

In contrast to such lax, ineffective parenting, effective discipline embodies three principles. The first step is to clearly and unambiguously communicate to children what behavior is allowed and what is unacceptable. It is hard for children of permissive parents to know what they should and should not do because parental rules and prohibitions have not been clearly communicated. The second characteristic of effective discipline is that children must be told the consequences or punishment for breaking the rules. Third, and most important, the effective disciplinarian consistently follows through and enforces the rules. Permissively raised children quickly learn that they don't have to listen to their parents because they won't follow through.

Researchers have identified this highly effective disciplinary style as "authoritative." This third approach combines strict limits and reliably enforced rules, reasons and explanations for parental rules, high expectations for responsible and mature behavior, and much parental warmth and overtly expressed affection. Highly effective parents possess a wide range of parenting skills that allows them to combine firm discipline with nurturant child care.

The authoritative parent believes in strict discipline but, unlike the authoritarian parent, couples this with more physical affection and verbal approval. For example, the authoritative father demands obedience but also tells his children stories, rolls with them on the floor, holds them in his lap, praises them when they do well, and looks in their eyes and says, "I love you." Children more readily cooperate with requests from an affectionate parent than from one who is threatening or distant.

Although authoritative parents are firm about discipline, they also invite children's participation in the process. Children are encouraged to offer alternatives or compromise solutions that would be better to them but would still satisfy parents. Authoritative parents also tell their children what they would like them to do and explain why certain behavior is encouraged or discouraged. In contrast, the authoritarian parent provides clearly defined and enforced limits, but no room for compromise, alternatives, or explanations. Even very young children may be more willing to cooperate if they understand the reasons for the rules. Adult authority seems less arbitrary or unfair when children can participate in the discipline process.

Authoritative parents always enforce the rules they set. Permissive parents may offer reasons and explanations to lessen their children's disapproval, but ultimately they do not take a firm stance and rigorously enforce limits. Children are very astute judges of how serious their parents are about enforcing rules. If parents enforce rules inconsistently, children will continually try to break them. Thus, whether or not the child has been able to understand or agree, authoritative parents enforce the rules that have been set.

The authoritative parent exercises a wide range of parenting skills and combines the most effective features of the other two parenting styles. We have seen that the authoritarian parent sets limits but does so harshly, whereas the permissive parent does not place appropriate controls on children. Although parents believe that they have to be either strict or loving, authoritative parents have the flexibility to be effective in both ways. Despite the best of intentions, however, balancing these two domains is very hard for most parents. Authoritative child-rearing requires parents to have a broad enough personality to be both nurturing and emotionally available to children, while still being able to set rules and tolerate children's disapproval for enforcing them.

Authoritative parents also make the effort to talk with their children. They state the rules, explain why certain behavior is encouraged or discouraged, and entertain alternatives and compromises before they enforce the rules. Furthermore, these parents also expect mature, responsible behavior from their children. In order to do so successfully, authoritative parents must be able to accurately assess the upper level of children's abilities. Because children are constantly changing, it is difficult to determine what demands for mature and responsible behavior will challenge children yet allow them to succeed.

Although it is challenging for parents to provide this authoritative childrearing, it produces the most healthy, well-adjusted children. Researchers have found that children raised in this authoritative manner are independent, self-controlled, successful with friends, and have a positive outlook.

Discipline After Divorce

After divorce, most children are raised by single mothers, who often have significant child-rearing problems. Although children require clearer limits and more structured households during and after the divorce, custodial mothers often become more erratic and inconsistent in their discipline. Researchers have found that six years after divorce, many single mothers are ineffectual disciplinarians who give many instructions with little follow through. These mothers tended to nag and complain, but they allowed children to interrupt often and frequently gave in or yielded to children's demands. Especially with sons, many single mothers are angry, short-tempered, and punitive. In addition to problems with discipline and control, these custodial mothers also communicate less with their children and are less supportive and nurturant.

Ineffective child-rearing practices lead to child adjustment problems, not the divorce, as is so often heard. Because boys in particular, but girls as well, tend to respond to the stress of divorce with more active, disobedient, and aggressive behavior, children of divorce require effective authoritative parenting. Parental affection and firm but responsive control is essential for children's positive adjustment to divorce. Children of divorce, especially boys, will also adjust better in authoritative schools with explicitly defined schedules, clear rules and regulations, consistent but understanding discipline, and expectations for mature behavior.

Single parents should try to adopt the authoritative approach with their children because the problems with the authoritarian and permissive modes only increase after divorce. Children are more likely to defy the authoritarian father because they are angry at him for leaving the family and because he no longer holds the same authority in the family that he did before the divorce. A mother may be more apt to be permissive because she cannot assume the disciplinary role the father used to have. It will be especially difficult for her to enforce rules if she needs her children's approval too much during this stressful period. Thus, even though children need effective, authoritative parenting during and after divorce, it is difficult to provide. Four factors make effective parenting more challenging after divorce.

First, discipline is harder in the first year after the separation because changes in family relationships cause children to be more restless and insecure. To feel safer and more secure, children begin to push rules and limits their parents have set in order to test boundaries and elicit firm controls. Children test to see if their parents are going to remain dependably in control of them. Divorcing parents must keep in mind that firm, consistent discipline is an essential source of security and stability for children as they adjust to new family relations.

Second, children may be less cooperative with parental discipline because they are angry. As noted in chapter 6, school-aged boys are especially likely to respond to marital separation with anger and defiance. Often, children will be angry at the father for leaving but express this anger toward the mother because she is available. Most boys and girls, however, will become more demanding and disobedient following the breakup, which makes them harder to discipline.

Third, changes in the mother's life also contribute to the discipline problem. As detailed in chapter 6, the father generally handles most of the discipline of sons. After the marital separation, the single mother often must take on this new role of disciplinarian. Escalating wars often occur between single mothers and sons that make life miserable for both. Mothers are frustrated as they fail to control their angry and disobedient sons and, as a result, become more critical, punitive, and unsupportive of them. In turn, these sons become even more provocative, uncommunicative, and disobedient, so that mothers feel more out of control and more like failures as parents. Because this vicious circle just intensifies, it is essential for these single mothers to attend parenting classes and get the help they need to regain control.

Finally, the father's ability to control his children also tends to diminish following divorce because he usually spends less time with his children and, as a result, has less influence over them. Even when he remains actively involved, however, children are often less responsive to his attempts at discipline than they were before the separation. And, if the father becomes more interested in winning the children's approval than in enforcing the rules—as often happens—children will receive even less of the discipline and guidance they need.

Thus, several factors converge to make discipline more of a problem following separation: the children are harder to manage, the mother is trying to assume new parental responsibilities, and the father's authority is declining. These circumstances each contribute to less effective discipline, which in turn leads to behavior problems in the children. As attempts to set limits and establish controls fail at home, children begin to have problems at school as well. Thus, the issue of effective discipline becomes one of the most important problems facing divorcing families.

Child-Rearing Guidelines for Divorced Parents

Discipline

In almost every family—intact, single-parent, or step-family—discipline is the parents' foremost concern. I once asked forty mothers and fathers to write down their most important parenting problem and thirty-nine responses focused on the issue of discipline. Many parents report that it is difficult to get their children to mind them and, as we have just seen, these problems with discipline only increase after marital disruption. However, children need their parents to provide firm, consistent discipline that is not angry, threatening, or demeaning. According to researchers, the healthiest children grow up with clearly defined and regularly enforced rules coupled with warmth and affection. Researchers have also found that if parents do not effectively discipline them, children of divorce are far more likely to develop personality and adjustment problems than children of divorce who are effectively disciplined.

CHILDREN REQUIRE WARM BUT FIRM DISCIPLINE. Positive adjustment in children depends on parental control because children feel safer and more secure when parents effectively discipline them. Children want their parents to take charge of them by setting and enforcing realistic rules; they become calmer, more secure, and happier when parents are in control. Parents often ask, if children want their parents to be in charge, why do they push limits and disobey rules? Children disobey to test how serious their parents are about enforcing the rules. Children know they are not safe and cannot depend on the adult to take care of them unless they are certain that their parents are in charge.

INEFFECTIVE DISCIPLINE FOLLOWING DIVORCE. Because of the stress of divorce, many parents feel insecure and begin to question their judgment. Often these parents, who had been relatively effective disciplinarians before the divorce, come to rely too much on their child's approval of them. These parents are too threatened by their children's anger or criticism, and children soon learn that they can use this vulnerability to manipulate parents and escape rules and limits.

These parents do not discipline effectively because they are afraid of their children's rejection if they take a firm stand and say no. Because the parents' need for acceptance is heightened, they stop enforcing limits as soon as their children become angry or critical. These parents no longer see their children's complaints as merely predictable attempts to evade what they don't want to do; instead, they take their children's criticism as true statements about who they are. When this occurs, children have been given too much control over their parents' sense of well-being. As a result, these parents plead with their children, rather than telling them, to go to bed at night, for example. Parent and child both begin to suffer when control shifts from the parent to the child.

As these insecure, approval-seeking parents become more permissive after the divorce, their children become angrier, more demanding, and increasingly disrespectful. Before long, the parents feel out of control as children ignore, complain, or argue with every parental request. The parent–child relationship becomes a chronic battle for control. Especially when the parents have grown up in highly authoritarian families, they become increasingly passive and compliant— defeated in the face of their children's obnoxious behavior. The defeat does not usually last very long, however, as exasperated parents resort to the worst features of their own authoritarian upbringings. These parents become critical, angry, and punitive toward their children. They begin to carp, nag, and criticize everything their children do, and can no longer acknowledge positive behavior. They frequently shout and make demands that they never enforce. These parents have swung from being too permissive to being ineffectively authoritarian. They are unsupportive, demanding, and threatening, but fail to uphold rules and make children obey. In the years following divorce, researchers describe many single mothers and sons, in particular, who are locked into this power battle that makes life miserable for parent and child. To break this vicious cycle, parents must begin to exercise more authoritative control.

EFFECTIVE DISCIPLINE. Effective disciplinarians begin by rewarding children's positive behavior. When children dress themselves, take out the trash, share toys, say thank you, or sleep through the night, parents should reward this good behavior with smiles, praise, hand clapping, touching, winks, and so on. Authoritarian parents, who are reluctant to affirm their children when they behave well, make the mistake of only responding to problem behavior. Children obey better when they are appreciated for what they do well and when they feel loved.

In order to discipline effectively, parents must also be able to communicate clearly and directly what they expect of their children. Permissive parents fail to give children clear expectations for what they should and should not do. Their children are not well-behaved, in part because they do not know what is expected of them. For example, when such a child misbehaves by hitting a younger sister, permissive parents give vague corrections such as, "Why are you hitting your sister again? Come on, that's not very nice." In response to this unclear directive, the child does not know what to do.

Alternatively, there is another type of ineffectively authoritarian parent who always barks commands at children but does not enforce them. These parents, who are angry and often criticize or embarrass their children, can easily become embroiled in coercive cycles. In the case of the child hitting a younger sister, such parents would shout, "Knock it off right now! What's wrong with you? Can't you ever get along with anyone?" In this case, the parent communicates that the child should stop hitting, but this central message is lost in the additional threatening and demeaning messages. Because they shout, threaten, and spank repeatedly, these parents provide a role model of someone who is irrational, upset, and out of control—behavior their children imitate. Negative coercive cycles also escalate as children learn that they have the power to provoke their parents. Knowing they do not have to respect or obey, these children often continue to taunt and elicit parental outbursts.

In contrast, the authoritative parent communicates more clearly and directly with the child. For example, such a parent who sees a child hitting a younger sister immediately gives simple, direct commands. The parent walks over to the child, bends over to make close eye contact, has a stern facial expression, addresses the child by name, and in a calm, firm voice gives a single directive: "John, stop hitting her." If the child does not obey, the parent backs up commands with immediate consequences, such as time-out.

Parents must find ways to effectively control their children without resorting to intimidation through physical violence, ridicule, and shame and without threats of leaving or abandoning them. Time-out is the most effective discipline method parents can employ. It allows parents to be effectively in control and stop unwanted behavior without displaying agitation or anger.

How does time-out work? In a nutshell, parents must first select two or three specific behaviors they want to focus on stopping—for example, temper tantrums, using profanity, biting, climbing on furniture, hitting, or talking back. Parents then locate the place in the house that is most boring for their child; it should be away from other people, the TV, toys, and other stimulation. (For example, the bathroom is suitable for a ten-year-old, or a chair in the corner of a room for a three-year-old.) Parents should explain the time-out program to their children in advance. When the targeted misbehavior next occurs, the parent places the child in the time-out place. The parent sends the child to time-out *using no more than ten words* (no arguments, no lectures) and *no longer than ten seconds* after the targeted misbehavior occurs (you cannot give time-out for misbehavior that you observed five minutes earlier). Thus, the next time the child hits a younger sister, the parent responds immediately by saying, "You have time-out for hitting your sister," and taking the child to the time-out location.

Time-out should last one minute for each year of the child's age—two minutes for two-year-olds, ten minutes for ten-year-olds, and so on. Parents should set a portable egg timer when the child goes into time-out and should not interact with the child again until the timer rings. When the timer rings, children know that time-out is over and must tell the parent why they were sent to time-out. For example, the parent can say, "The timer has rung. Why did you have time-out?" The child might respond, "I hit my sister." The parent can then reply, "Yes, you had time-out for hitting your sister. Time-out is over now." If the child leaves time-out or creates a ruckus while there, the parent restarts the timer. After the timer has rung and the child has stated the reason for being put in time-out, the incident is over. The parent does not scold, lecture, withdraw emotionally, or remain angry at the child; instead, everyone returns to normal activities.

Parents cannot use time-out to make children initiate good behavior or do what they do not want to (for example, clean their rooms, do their homework), but it is remarkably effective in stopping undesirable behavior in a short time. Before beginning a time-out program, parents need more preparation than we can cover in this book to handle complications that may arise (for example, if the child refuses to go to or remain in the time-out location). Although there are many good books on time-out and other methods of discipline, *The Time-Out Solution* by Dr. L. Clark (Contemporary Books, 1989) is excellent reading for all parents who are struggling to remain in control of their children.

In addition to time-out, effective disciplinarians employ many other management strategies. At times, they may actively ignore children who are misbehaving. For example, if a young child is whining or having a temper tantrum, it is often effective to turn away and act absorbed in another activity or to simply walk out of the room. The parent must avoid eye contact with the misbehaving child and must not look angry or frustrated, or the maneuver will not succeed. Children are rewarded when they can provoke parents and will continue to do so as long as they can succeed. As soon as the misbehavior stops, parents must be sure to turn their positive attention back to the child for a minute or two. This final step is essential if this approach is to work.

Effective disciplinarians also use natural consequences, although this is more effective for school-aged than younger children. A natural consequence is the result that naturally follows from a child's misbehavior. Some examples of natural consequences are pushing another child and getting pushed back, not sharing with a friend so that the friend goes home, playing rough with a toy and then breaking it, or not getting to school on time and having to stay after. Some parents enable children to escape the natural consequences of their misbehavior by telling the other child to stop pushing back, allowing another friend to come over, buying a replacement toy right away, or asking the teacher to let the child go out to play. However, parents must not protect children from the real-life consequences of their behavior. Such protected children often become arrogant, demanding, selfish, insensitive to others, and less capable of sustained work. Authoritative parents allow children to experience the consequences of their behavior without intervening to rescue them.

In many situations, of course, parents cannot use this approach. When natural consequences are too serious or dangerous (for example, riding a bicycle in the street), parents can use logical consequences, which are punishments that logically fit the child's misbehavior. For example, if a child rides a bicycle in the street, it is put away for four days; if a child does not brush his or her teeth, no desserts or sweets are allowed until brushing is resumed; if a child does not do homework, the television or telephone is turned off until it is completed. In this way, logical consequences follow directly from the child's misbehavior. Parents should communicate these consequences clearly and firmly, but without anger, rejection, or emotional withdrawal. Furthermore, when enforcing these consequences, parents must not become embroiled in arguments or justifications that only allow children to escape immediate consequences.

Finally, effective parents often avoid the need to discipline by anticipating situations that are likely to arouse problems. For example, when they take children grocery shopping in the late afternoon, parents first give them a snack so they do not feel hungry and demand sweets in the store. Or, when they walk in the door after a long day at work, such parents don't answer the telephone or make long telephone calls until they have spent time with each child. Or, when several children are playing indoors and fighting or rough-and-tumble begins, parents intervene before things begin to escalate. Such parents provide children with more direction and structure at these critical moments by initiating building projects with blocks, putting together puzzles, or beginning drawing projects to focus children's play. In planning and organizing in these ways, parents can prevent many potential discipline problems.

TEMPERAMENT. Finally, children's temperament is an important aspect of the discipline issue. Every grandmother knows that some children are innately harder to raise than others, and researchers have given scientific backing to this folk wisdom by identifying a number of biologically based behavioral styles or temperamental characteristics that make some children easier to raise and others more difficult.

In the first few years of life, some children are found to be more irritable, more difficult to soothe when distressed, more fearful of new people and places, more active, more intense in their emotional responses, and more irregular in their biological rhythms of feeding, sleeping, and eliminating. These children, who are more often boys than girls, are temperamentally more difficult for many parents. Such children are not bad in any way—they are simply born with certain physiological characteristics that make them more demanding or challenging for most parents to raise.

For example, suppose a young, new mother has a baby that cries readily and is not easily soothed. Although this mother is just as capable as the mother next door who has a temperamentally easier child, she is likely to feel inadequate because her baby cries a great deal and she cannot do anything about it. And what if her baby is also very active and intense in his emotional responses? Negative cycles often begin to escalate as the mother's feelings of frustration and inadequacy lead her to either anger and rejection toward the child or to depression and withdrawal. Unfortunately, either response will only increase the child's crying. Furthermore, if the baby also has very irregular biological rhythms, this mother will have additional troubles because it will be difficult for her to plan her day and carve out time for herself as she doesn't know when her child will be hungry or want a nap. This exasperated young mother will not be able to find much-needed relief from this loud, "demanding" baby, and as a result, she may become further frustrated and short-tempered with him, and even more discouraged about her adequacy as a mother. Sadly, before too long many parents in this situation begin to think of their child as "bad" and respond accordingly.

It is easy to see how children's difficult temperaments can lead to escalating negative cycles between parents and children. Problems in parent–child interaction that start in the first few years of life often are later expressed in behavior problems as children become school-aged. Researchers have found that the majority of children referred to child guidance clinics for therapy are boys with difficult temperaments. Again, it should be stressed that the temperament itself is not the problem. Some parents enjoy their active and intense children, do not need predictable daily schedules, are patient in helping children warm up slowly to new activities, and are sympathetic rather than frustrated by their children's fussiness. These parents often think that their child has "character" or a "strong personality" and will grow up to be an interesting person—and they are right. For many other parents, however, the same temperamental characteristics lead to problems in parent–child interaction, so that children are regarded as "bad," a characterization that becomes a self-fulfilling prophecy as behavior problems develop that require professional help.

Unfortunately, this problematic sequence does not stop with the parent–child relationship; in most cases, it gradually pulls in the marital relationship as well. Researchers have found that families with temperamentally difficult children have more marital conflict than families with temperamentally easier children. The on-going conflict between the parent and child creates more stress in the marriage, and researchers have shown that parents with temperamentally difficult children are also more likely to divorce.

Tragically, this harmful sequence continues in the years following the divorce, when temperamentally difficult children are more likely to be the target of single parents' frustration and stress than temperamentally easier children. Researchers find that many single mothers in particular are embroiled in on-going control battles with temperamentally difficult sons. When parents and children become locked in chronic battling, parents must get help to stop this runaway cycle and regain control. Parents can learn about effective authoritative discipline by reading books such as *The Time-Out Solution* (cited previously) and parenting books on child temperament such as *Know Your Child* (Chess, Alexander, and Thomas, Basic Books, 1987). Parent education classes organized by the local YWCA, public school, daycare center, or church also teach parents to take charge more effectively.

Child-Rearing Problems in Shared Parenting Households

One of the most common child-rearing concerns expressed by divorcing parents is what will happen to a child asked to conform to one set of rules at the mother's house and another set at the father's. As noted in chapter 8, it is best if the mother and father can talk together and agree on common rules, standards, and child-rearing practices. In many cases, however, parents will have differing beliefs and values about child-rearing. However, children can adjust to two different ways of doing things if the rules are clearly communicated to them and consistently enforced within each household. As long as children know what is expected of them within each home, they are flexible enough to adapt. For example, a mother can say to her child, "It's 8:30 and time for you to go to bed." If the child protests, she can continue, "I know that you don't have a bedtime at your father's house, but you know the rules are different here. Would you like me to read you a story before you go to sleep?"

However, problems are likely to arise if one parent enforces the rules and the other parent is lax. When children are permissively raised and can escape consequences in one household, they will be highly motivated to push the limits to test how much they can get away with in the other household. The parent who is trying to provide a predictable home environment, with clearly defined limits and regularly enforced consequences, will be challenged intensely by these children, especially in the beginning. Parents in this situation must expect extensive testing by children and must be resilient enough to weather the storm for a while. Eventually children learn that the parent means business and will stay in charge, even though things are looser at their other home. Gradually, children will stop disobeying and defying the parent when their attempts are repeatedly met by firmness.

Without question, though, it is difficult for the responsible parent in this scenario to stick to the rules. Initially, children will threaten by expressing preference for the more permissive parent. Over time, however, most children prefer to be with a firm but supportive parent. Often too, the responsible parent resents having to be "the heavy" and begins to give in too often in order to escape this uncomfortable role. Finally, it is also fatiguing for responsible parents to hold to their rules and enforce the consequences of breaking them during children's initial period of strong testing. Understandably, but unfortunately, many of these parents buckle under the combined weight of these pressures and stop providing the effective discipline their children need. Child behavior problems then begin to develop because children have no dependable control in either home. To prevent this result, the responsible parent should attempt to discuss this parenting problem with the permissive parent and a mediator. Child-rearing will be easier if this consultation is effective, but even if it isn't, children still adjust far better when one parent remains in control within one household.

Finally, significant child-rearing problems also occur in shared-parenting families when children can play one parent off against the other. When divorcing parents are combative, children use their conflicts to manipulate them and undermine effective discipline. Problems emerge when children receive support for disobeying the other parent or even when they merely have a supportive ear for complaining about the other parent's rules. For example, the mother will have trouble enforcing limits with her daughter if the child can successfully appeal to her father for support. If mother insists that daughter pick up her room at 8:15 P.M. and go to bed at 8:30, but father laughs at these rules and tells the daughter that she is old enough to set her own bedtime, the father has given the daughter permission to disobey her mother.

In their readiness to continue their conflicts with the former spouse, combative parents undermine the parenting authority of the other parent and allow children to escape the consequences of their behavior. Commonly, these parents do so by drawing a parallel between their own conflicts with the former spouse and the discipline-related problems the child is having with the other parent. For example, whenever eleven-year-old George complained to his mother that his father insisted he do his homework every night, his mother reassured, "Yes, I know, your Dad was always rigid and controlling with me, too." In turn, of course, his father complained to George about his mother's "lack of standards" and tried to control what George did at her house. George quickly learned how to get the responses he wanted at both his mother's and his father's house. As a result, George had no effective discipline in either household.

What happens to children like George who can play their parents off against each other and escape the consequences of their behavior? In a word, they become manipulative. Such children learn that rules apply to others, not to them, so they will disobey teachers and rules whenever they think they can get away with it. These children also become opportunistic and manipulatively please those in power for their own immediate gains. Because of their grace and charm, they often successfully ingratiate themselves with teachers and popular peers. Oriented to power, prestige, and attention, these children may be verbally skilled, well dressed, and top performers in high-status activities such as dancing. Despite having such popularity, however, their relationships are superficial—they have short-lived friendships and no enduring close friends.

As adults, their manipulativeness, self-centeredness, and reluctance to accept limits are likely to lead to problems in work, where adults must be able to conform to rules, accept responsibility, and cooperate with others. Their ability to manipulate others and avoid consequences also leads to impulsive acting out, and they are more likely than others to become involved with alcohol and drugs. Combative parents must recognize that when they allow children to avoid legitimate discipline by playing them off against each other, significant problems will follow.

Meeting Children's Needs for Love and Attention

We have already seen that children have increased needs for love and affection in responses to the upheaval of family disruption.

Their initial reaction to their parents' breakup includes profound anxiety and insecurity that they will try to cope with by eliciting reassurance from all the adults in their world. They will want to be held and read to, to have their hair brushed and to have endless questions answered. These are predictable reactions to divorce, and parents should help their children cope by accepting and responding to these increased needs for attention.

Boys as well as girls will have these heightened needs. As noted in chapter 6, some divorcing parents accept their daughters' demands for attention but are reluctant to meet these same needs in their sons. Our cultural stereotypes ignore the fact that little boys feel sad, want to be held, and suffer from the same pain and fear as girls when parents part. These feelings are often derided as "sissy," dependent or weak in boys, which is one reason why most young boys have more trouble adjusting to divorce than girls.

Although divorcing parents should try to be more affectionate and supportive with their children, what about parents' ability to respond to these increased needs? Previous chapters have already emphasized that divorce is also a stressful time for parents. Mothers and fathers must cope with new living arrangements, financial worries, and their own losses. It's often hard for newly single parents to find enough time or emotional energy to respond to their children's increased demands. Thus, unfortunately, children often receive less affection and attention in the first year following the separation—just at the time they need it most. Many parents feel guilty about not being able to meet their children's needs, and this guilt may intensify doubts about the decision to divorce, so that an unproductive cycle of self-recrimination and depression is perpetuated in the parent.

How can this twofold problem of increased child need and decreased parental availability be resolved? First, parents must establish their own emotional support systems. You cannot effectively nurture your children if you are not doing anything for yourself. Realistically, the demands of single-parenting are too great to fulfill without sympathetic and responsive others who can be relied on for support, sharing, and information. Parents can begin to create a support network for themselves through organizations such as Parents Without Partners, church groups, the YWCA, or parent groups that form in connection with quality childcare programs.

Having established some ways to take care of themselves, parents can begin to provide three- to nine-year-old children with a regularly scheduled "special time." Parents can set aside specific times every week to be alone with the child. For example, every Monday and Thursday night from 7:00 to 7:30, and every Saturday from 4:00 to 4:30, Johnny is scheduled to have his mother all to himself. They will still be together at many other times during the week, but Johnny knows that he can have his mother's complete attention during these special periods. Children like having these predictable half hours with their parent, and this special time will have a stabilizing effect on them.

Once children learn that they can always rely on having the time that has been set aside for them, they will be better able to accept those times when parents must put them off. For example, when Johnny is demanding his mother's attention as she is leaving for work, his mother can respond: "I know you would really like me to be with you right now, but I have to go to work. Today is Monday and we will have our special time tonight at 7:00. We can be together then. Let me give you a hug for now and tonight will be our special time just for you and me." Special time can lessen many conflicts over the need for more time and affection.

Parents should use this period as an opportunity to do several important things with their child. Some ground rules follow.

1. This parent–child time should be spent in a room with the door shut to prevent all interruptions. Do not answer the phone or turn on the television during this special time. Instead, read a favorite story together or play a game of the child's choosing. The idea is for the parent to give the child undivided attention and follow the child's wishes and interests as much as possible. (For example, "What would you like to do together now?")

2. During the special time, parents should tell children they love them and how much they enjoy being with them. For example, "I am really glad we have this time when just you and I can be together. I like it when we can be close and have fun together like this. Do you know how much I miss you when I am away at work?"

3. The parent must praise the child for at least one thing he or she has done recently that the parent appreciated or took pride in. For example, "I was really proud of you for helping your sister with her homework last night." Even if you are thinking about the six

things your child has just done that you didn't like, use this time to acknowledge what you have appreciated.

4. Save discussion of discipline problems or other causes of parental unhappiness for another time. This period is a time for affection, sharing, and play.

5. The child should be touched, rubbed, and hugged during every session. Even if this seems awkward or unnatural to you, do it anyway. Your child will be hungry for your affection and such gestures will soon become natural.

This kind of affectionate and attentive parent–child interaction often does as much to alleviate a child's problems and to reduce parent–child conflict as anything that can be done by parents, teachers, or therapists. Parents who reliably provide their children with special time and carry out the guidelines I have suggested will have fewer behavior problems to cope with. Try it for one month, two nights per week, and evaluate the results for yourself—they are often startling. Of course, by itself, special time is not enough. Parents also need to set aside predictable times every day to be with the child. For example, parents can set the alarm fifteen minutes earlier to be with the child at the beginning of the day or can arrange a special time alone with the child before bedtime. This type of affectionate daily contact, coupled with special time, can go a long way toward meeting children's needs.

Finally, some parents feel too awkward to tell their children that they love them, are uncomfortable with close physical contact, or cannot think of positive things the child has done. These problems stem from their own relationships with their parents. Parents unwittingly repeat the limitations of their own parents with their children. I encourage parents who have difficulty expressing affection and approval to seek counseling and learn how they can become more caring and affirming with their children than their parents were with them. Once unresolved problems in their own childhoods are honestly acknowledged, it is not very hard for parents to learn new and better ways to nurture their children. Although the process does require acknowledging some painful feelings, and parents may feel guilty—as if they are somehow betraying their parents by realistically acknowledging limitations—this relearning can make life far richer for parent and child alike.

Giving Structure and Organization to Children's Lives

Young children of divorce will adjust better if parents structure their lives with predictable daily routines. As adults, most of us find it boring to have the same schedule every day. We look forward to weekends and vacations when we don't have to plan what we are going to do next, but children are different in this respect. Children find security in a predictable schedule, and they are made anxious by too much freedom.

It is hard for young children to make sense of their world and understand what happens to them. Because young children do not have the emotional or intellectual capacity to take control of their environment and order their own world, they depend upon adults to filter their experiences and make the world manageable. Without adult structuring, children can be overwhelmed by their experiences. If parents can provide an orderly and predictable environment, children will be calm and secure enough to explore and learn. It is a romantic notion to think of children as carefree and creative beings who can effortlessly float through a day's activities. Especially as a response to the stress of divorce, children welcome a predictable daily routine and a smoothly organized household.

Researchers have found that children of divorce who have a more organized home environment are better adjusted than those living in less structured homes. A theme we have touched on before merits mentioning again: Some single parents are so stressed by the pain and disruption of divorce and the enormous demands of being a single parent that their ability to provide a predictable family environment is diminished. It is hard to plan a family's activities and make sure that this schedule is followed when you are feeling overwhelmed. Most divorcing parents take a year or more to regain control of their lives and effectively organize daily family routines after the separation. The longer this adjustment takes, however, the more problems children will have in coping with their redefined family following the divorce.

Divorcing parents should strive to organize their children's day into a predictable routine. Children should know where they are going, what they will be doing, and who they will be with each day. Breaks in this schedule should be minimized and, when they occur, children should be informed of the changes in advance. As much as possible, children should also know when they have to go to bed, when lunch will be served, and what time parents will be coming and going from the home. It will also help if children know when they will be bathed, what time they can watch TV, and what they have to do to prepare for school each day. Children of all ages should have household responsibilities that they are regularly expected to perform, such as setting the table, carrying dishes to the kitchen, emptying trash, sweeping walks, and completing homework.

All of these activities can be used to establish a predictable daily schedule. Although this structure may sound rigid to some parents, children feel more free within an orderly, familiar routine. They are more confident and they feel more in control when they know what to expect. This predictable home life, coupled with effective discipline and affectionate caring, helps ensure children's healthy adjustment.

11

Step-Families: Forming New Family Relationships

Step-families are the fastest growing type of family in the United States. Although the divorce rate is high, people have not given up on marriage. Approximately one-half of all adults who divorce remarry within one year, and seventy-five percent of women and eighty percent of men remarry within three years. Despite somewhat lower remarriage rates for adults who have children, most people continue to seek a partner in life. As a result of this high remarriage rate, about one out of every four children will spend some time living with a stepparent. In this final chapter, we look ahead to the problems children face when their parents remarry.

The Bias Against Step-Families

Step-families have an undeservedly bad reputation as problem-ridden or unnatural families that are not as good as "real" or nuclear families. This attitude is probably an extension of the stigma of divorce. Prejudice against step-families is clearly seen in the wicked stepmother myth that still flourishes. Cinderella and Snow White taught us long ago that stepmothers are selfish, cold, and cruel. However, it is unfair to see stepparents as villains; it is time they received some support.

Stepchildren, too, are sometimes viewed as living in second-class families. One of the tasks of a step-family is to overcome these unfortunate stereotypes and create a positive family identify. The step-family can be a rich and satisfying family form, although it is very different from the original, non-divorced or nuclear family, and problems must be addressed in building a successful step-family.

Children's Reactions to Step-Family Formation

Children entering step-families face two primary problems. First, it is very hard for children to accept that a new spouse is joining their family. Children often feel that the new spouse is replacing their other parent and so they resist this change. In particular, school-aged children and adolescents are usually very cool toward this "substitute" for their natural parent. Thus loyalty conflicts are aroused by the remarriage, and they will be especially intense when the natural parents do not get along. Even if their natural parents are cooperative, however, children still fear that they are betraying their other parent if they accept the new spouse. Parents and stepparents must keep in mind that, regardless of how infrequently children see the other parent or of how ineffective or irresponsible that parent has been, children still need to safeguard and preserve aspects of their relationship with the other parent. Wise parents will accept and affirm their children's need to keep alive their ties to their biological parents. Adults should not pressure children to acknowledge problems with their natural parent or to accept the new stepparent within the first two years.

Out of allegiance to the other parent, most children will initially reject new spouses and prevent stepparents from feeling that they belong to the family. For example, children do this by calling a biological parent at work for permission, even when the stepparent is at home; telling a stepparent that only a "real" parent can sign a school permission slip; informing the stepparent that their real parent does something a different way; telling stepparents about good times when the biological family was together and they were a "real" family; or, most blatantly of all, making direct verbal accusations such as, "You're not my dad!"

It is easy for those outside the family to appreciate why children feel threatened by the new spouse. However, it is not so easy to be understanding when you are receiving the brunt of children's anger and rejection. It is hard for most adults when children only speak to the natural parent, constantly intrude on adult conversations, and refuse the interest and overtures of the stepparent.

The second problem for stepchildren is the fear of losing their parent to the new spouse. Children have already suffered a loss through the marital breakup and they will be highly sensitized to further perceived losses. From children's perspective, the remarriage is at first an unwanted loss of their parent rather than the gain of a stepparent, especially because close parent–child relationships develop in many single-parent families. The remarriage brings another adult into this tightly woven unit and threatens to break up the strong alliances that developed while parent and child lived alone together. Children feel displaced by the intrusion and try to keep their parent for themselves. In addition, children may not feel that there is "enough" of mother or father to go around if they have to share their parent with a new spouse. Unwilling to give up any of their parent's attention and affection, most children will be jealous, competitive, and rejecting toward the new spouse in the beginning.

Largely because of these two factors, there is usually a high level of family conflict during the first two years of the remarriage. It often takes this long to resolve these significant issues and establish a more harmonious equilibrium. As we have seen in other situations, however, age and gender differences also play an important part in determining how children adjust to remarriage.

Although boys have more trouble adjusting to divorce and to life in a single-mother home, with remarriage, the picture changes. Girls usually have more difficulty adjusting to the introduction of a stepparent than boys. Why is remarriage so much harder for girls? Sons can gain something from a stepfather if he is warm and supportive. As described in chapter 6, most sons have little contact with their natural fathers in the years following the divorce. In addition, sons are often embroiled in angry, coercive control battles with their mothers while living as a single-parent family. If their stepfathers are emotionally responsive, most sons will gradually accept their interest and a mutually satisfying relationship will develop. Several years after remarriage, researchers have found that sons with nurturant stepfathers are better adjusted than sons in single-mother homes and that they are as well adjusted as sons in intact families.

Unlike sons, however, daughters usually have something to lose from the addition of a stepfather. Girls tend to cope with the initial marital breakup better than boys and function better in single-mother homes. Powerful mother–daughter ties often develop in such households, and these close ties are threatened by the remarriage. The daughter is often especially close to her mother and may be her mother's confidante and friend. Most daughters are very reluctant to relinquish their special status (although this tie can be problematic for daughters in the long run) and accept a new stepfather. As a result of this threatened displacement, the level of conflict between parents and stepdaughters becomes as high as it was between divorced mothers and sons in single-mother families. Unfortunately, whereas the high level of initial conflict between sons and stepparents usually diminishes, the level often remains high for stepdaughters years after the remarriage. Thus, most stepfathers will eventually be able to adopt an active parenting role with sons but will continue to be rejected by the stepdaughter.

In addition to these significant gender differences, age is also an important factor in step-family formation. In general, the younger the children are at the time of remarriage, the more easily they will adjust to the new stepparent. Researchers have found that preadolescence is an especially stressful age for remarriage. Almost all stepparents will fail to be accepted by nine- to twelve-year-old stepchildren. In particular, children's concerns about their own awakening sexuality seems to make even modest displays of affection between the new couple unacceptable. In contrast, older adolescents, who are future oriented and preparing to leave home, often adjust more easily to the new stepparent.

Three Styles of Stepparenting

Largely in response to children's ages, most stepparents will fall into one of three different styles of stepparenting: a primary parent, other parent, and an older friend.

Parents with young children who remarry can establish a step-family that is very similar to the nuclear family, and the stepparent can become one of the primary parents. Young children readily develop a close attachment to a responsive stepparent. As a result, a stepparent can take on a traditional parent role with children under about eight years of age. Stepparents can often nurture and discipline stepchildren as if they were their own in only a few months' time, and children may call these stepparents Mom or Dad and fully accept them as parents. Primary stepparenting is more common when the other biological parent is uninvolved and when children are younger. This is usually the most harmonious step-family.

The most common form of stepparenting, and the most difficult, is as the other parent. This style usually occurs when children have a continuing relationship with their other biological parent and they are nine to fifteen years old. Children at these ages are especially likely to reject or antagonize the new stepparent, especially during the first one to two years of the remarriage. As a result, most children who are nine to fifteen years old when their parent remarries will not accept mothering or fathering from a stepparent. Daughters, in particular, have a very difficult time accepting the authority of a new stepmother or stepfather. In the beginning, the natural parent must retain primary responsibility for parenting, and stepparents should only move into the parent role gradually. In this case, it will be easier for children to accept the new stepparent's authority over time. Tremendous conflicts ensue whenever the natural parent tries to leave parental responsibilities for nurturing or disciplining children to the new stepparent.

Stepparenting in the role of the other parent is challenging, indeed. Being an effective other parent requires effective family communication, support from your spouse, and the patience to develop your own relationships with children. In contrast, the third stepparenting style of friend is far easier. Stepparents who are friends may become important influences in children's lives, but they do so through the personal relationships they develop with children over time, not by filling a parental role. Older children and adoldescents usually prefer this friend role and often call stepparents by their first names. These step-families are relatively harmonious because children's ties to the noncustodial natural parent are not threatened, and control battles with the stepparent over authority and power are avoided.

The roles that stepparents play with stepchildren often change over time. An adult may fulfill all three stepparenting styles with one child over time or enact different roles with different stepchildren. With these three general stepparenting styles in mind, let's look more specifically at the issues confronting stepmothers and stepfathers.

Becoming Stepparents

STEPMOTHERS. Honestly stated, it is very difficult to become a stepmother. A woman who marries a man with custody of his children will probably encounter a great deal of conflict. These pressures often place the stepmother in an impossible bind.

To begin with, many stepmothers have unrealistic expectations of themselves. Initially, they often want to make up to the children for all of the pain they suffered from the divorce. New stepmothers also want to prove that they are not the wicked stepmother portrayed in all of the fairy tales. And, all too often, they fruitlessly try to create happy, close nuclear families. Stepmothers usually work hard to achieve these goals by sacrificing themselves to try to please everyone in the family.

These self-imposed pressures are intensified because others often hold unrealistic expectations for stepmothers as well. For example, stepmothers may be expected to automatically love their husband's children. The traditional female sex role dictates that she provide this loving maternal behavior, even though she is almost certain to be rejected by her new stepchildren. As a woman and wife, she is also supposed to nurture and provide daily care for her husband's children. If she cannot do this, she is considered to be a poor wife or mother and an inadequate woman. These expectations are unrealistic for most women and cause tremendous conflict in stepfamilies.

How do older children respond if their new stepmother tries to assume a mothering role? Out of loyalty to their natural mother and competition for their father, most children will reject the stepmother's attempts to be close, to take care of them, or to fill any of their mother's old role. In the process, children also tend to idealize their natural mother and actively attempt to make the stepmother feel lacking in comparison.

What happens to stepmothers when children rebuff them? Most keep trying to prove their affection and good intentions, but only continue to be rejected. Thus the stepmother is in a no-win situation. If she complies with cultural expectations and attempts to become the good mother and win the children's love and approval, she will have to submit to rejection and ridicule. And, at the same time, she will put her stepchildren in a position of great power and control over her. Substantial problems result for children and adults alike whenever this occurs.

Eventually, the children's rejection produces hurt and anger. This stepmother often goes through a period of anger at everyone: her new husband's former spouse, whose influence continues despite the remarriage; her husband, who spoils the children because he feels guilty about the divorce; and especially the stepchildren, who reject her and seem impossible to manage. The stepmother is now in a worse bind. Not only does she not like the children she is supposed to love, she resents them because they are ruining her life and making her fail as a homemaker and perhaps as a new wife as well.

This unhappy scenario occurs with great regularity. Soon after the marriage, many stepmothers who try to assume a primary parenting role begin to feel powerless, angry at the children, and abandoned by their husbands. As they begin to question their decision to marry, the level of conflict in the family starts to rise even higher. What is the solution to this scenario? Relationships between stepparents and stepchildren must develop over time—there is no instant love. All stepparents must be patient and have realistic expectations for how much affection or acceptance can occur in the first year or two. Before going on to examine this point further, let's look at the problems facing the new stepfather.

STEPFATHERS. It is easier to become a stepfather than a stepmother because men do not have the same cultural pressures to love and care for children. However, stepfathers have their own set of problems. Men are often expected to discipline children, and this role becomes a major problem in many step-families. In step-families, as in intact families, disciplining children is the foremost concern of parents.

Life will be very difficult for the new stepfather if he tries to assume a disciplinary role with older children within the first two years. Adults (especially the other natural parent) will hear constant complaints of injustice from the children, no matter how fair he is. In most cases, even the most sensitive and effective disciplinarian will be faced with outright defiance of his authority. A power struggle between stepfather and children ensues whenever stepfathers try to take on a disciplinary role soon after joining the family, and this conflict will make life miserable for everyone. In response to this initial failure and to children's reluctance to accept their friendly overtures, too many stepfathers give up on the children and disengage from them. They soon ignore the stepchildren and claim, "I married her, not the children." This withdrawal is very unfortunate because most stepfathers can become integrated into the family and develop meaningful relationships with children in a year or two.

There are many reasons why older children do not tolerate the stepfather's attempts to discipline them. First, they resent his assumption of their natural father's disciplinary role. Like absent natural mothers, the natural father is idealized, and the stepfather will receive the brunt of children's anger over the divorce and other problems he had little or nothing to do with.

Second, children do not want to obey someone they do not know or care about. Authority over children only grows out of investing time in developing a caring relationship with them. Stepfathers can eventually assume a disciplinary role, but they must do so over a period of years as they gradually develop personal relationships with the children. After about two years, most sons will accept—and even welcome—the stepfather's parenting role, although many daughters will not. Adolescents almost always resist the stepfather's discipline, however, and the mother will have to keep this responsibility.

Part of the discipline problem in some stepfamilies is that the stepfather receives conflicting messages from the mother. On the one hand, she may want him to share in the disciplinary role that she has had to carry alone. On the other hand, however, she may have become so closely allied with the children during her years as a single parent that she may not want to give up any of her control over them. Even mothers who are terribly tired of being responsible for discipline may find themselves resisting their new spouse's attempts to help. These common conflicting messages are upsetting and confusing to both adults. For the stepfather to succeed at parenting, however, the mother will have to support the stepfather in whatever actions he takes and clearly communicate to children that the stepfather is in charge when she is away.

Everyone involved in creating a step-family must bear in mind that complex changes in family alliances and roles will take place in the first two years after remarriage. All family members need to be patient during this challenging family reorganization.

Finding Solutions

The difficult transitions involved in creating a step-family can be eased in several ways. First, stepparents should not expect to love their new spouse's children. There is no need to apologize for or feel guilty about not loving someone else's children. It is a bonus if these positive feelings develop over time—and they often do—but they should not be expected. Children should be treated fairly and respectfully, but that is all that can realistically be asked for from stepparents. Once the onerous expectation to love each other has been shed, stepparents and stepchildren alike are free to enjoy each other's company.

Similarly, there is no need to try to win or earn children's affection. Problems often develop when stepparents feel they have to compete with their spouse's former spouse in order to gain stepchildren's love. Instead of spending more money, trying to be more fun, or struggling to be more understanding, be yourself and do not try to outdo the other parent. Courtesy and respect for the other parent is one of the best ways to end this competition.

Second, a step-family is formed because of the adults' interest in marrying each other, not because of the new spouse's interest in the children. The new spouse should not be expected to take on a parental role with the children—certainly not in the beginning and, with older children, perhaps never. Too many stepparents feel they have to fulfill traditional child-rearing roles, but they will face a great deal of conflict with older children and adolescents if they attempt to do so.

In the most harmonious step-families with older children and adolescents, the new spouse does not want to be a parent to the children and feels comfortable leaving this role to the natural parents. Although they can try to develop friendly relationships with them, they acknowledge the fact that their initial interest in the marriage was in the relationship with the spouse. Although this attitude may sound cold, it alleviates many stresses that occur in step-families: the children do not suffer from loyalty conflicts concerning their other natural parent and they are not worried about their natural parent being replaced. Furthermore, the stepparent is not placed in the untenable position of needing the children's approval or acceptance as a parent and does not enter into a losing battle over trying to make them obey.

As noted previously, one of the riskiest situations for step-families is when the natural parent wants the new marriage partner to take over parental responsibilities that he or she is having difficulty with. For example, a custodial father may expect his new wife to make sure that his adolescent daughter stops cutting classes and gets to school every day, after he goes to work. Or, a mother who has never liked to take a firm stand to make her twelve-year-old son do what she wants, may expect the stepfather to discipline him. However, these expectations are unrealistic and natural parents need to resolve their own parenting problems rather than handing over the conflict to stepparents. Unless the children are young, the natural parents should keep the parental role to themselves. For most stepparents, older friend is a better role than parent toward adolescents and toward all children in the beginning. When new spouses want to take a more active role, they should move slowly from the role of older friend to that of parent.

Forming a Successful Step-Family

Establishing a Primary Marital Coalition

The marital relationship is the primary axis in the step-family, just as it is in all two-parent families. The two biggest differences between well-functioning and problem-ridden step-families lie in the quality of the stepparent–stepchild relationship and in the nature of the marital partnership. The stability and cohesiveness of all other family relationships will be determined largely by the adults' ability to establish a marital coalition in which each partner feels supported by the other. We have already discussed the need for a primary marital coalition that cannot be disrupted by the demands of children and others. That need takes priority in stepfamilies, too, except that it is harder to establish a strong marital coalition in step-families than in nuclear families. Because the marital relationship is the key to successful family life and child-rearing, we should examine these difficulties closely.

The biggest obstacle for the new couple is having the children already present while they are trying to establish their own relationship. Unlike the couple in a nuclear family, the remarried couple does not have an exclusive spouse-to-spouse relationship before the children arrive. In chapter 8 we analyzed the developmental period of couple formation and showed that a newly married couple has a great deal of psychological work to do in building their relationship. Such things as establishing mutually agreeable patterns for their life together, agreeing on who makes decisions about money, and allocating how free time will be spent are all part of the process. How is the couple going to resolve differences of opinion and conflicts between them? What kind of balance will be struck when one spouse wants one thing but the other wants something different? The presence of children makes it harder to build a relationship as a couple and, too often, children become inappropriately involved in the marital relationship. One result is that the divorce rate is higher for remarriages (sixty percent) than first marriages. It is essential for the remarried couple to keep children and child-related concerns from constantly interfering with their relationship. Nothing is more important to the well-being of the new family.

The Martins are a blended family made up of "his, hers, and ours." The parents, Bob and Laura, are in their late thirties and have been married for four years. Bob was previously married and has two children, John, age ten, and Emma, age eight. John and Emma live with Bob and Laura four days a week, and with their mother, who lives nearby, the rest of the week. Laura has been divorced from her first husband for seven years. Her son, Ron, is nine, and her daughter, Leah, is seven. Both of her children live with Bob and Laura. Her former husband moved out of the state following the divorce and has had little contact with his children. Together, Bob and Laura also have one child, an eighteen-month-old toddler named Ross.

When Bob and Laura first began dating they found that they had a reasonable amount of time to enjoy each other, even when their children were present. The four older children were close in age, played well together, and soon became friends. After the wedding Bob and Laura were able to spend a week alone together before beginning their life as a family of six. Upon returning home from their honeymoon, however, the couple found that the children had changed.

As soon as Bob and Laura got married, Laura's children began to resist Bob's role as disciplinarian, and Bob's daughter, Emma, became very critical of Laura. Whereas the couple used to be able to be close together at home, now it was impossible for the newly- weds to have an uninterrupted moment. The children intruded whenever Bob and Laura tried to lock themselves away to get some privacy, and the two older children "erupted" whenever they were affectionate with each other. It seemed as if the children were joined in a conspiracy to keep them apart. As the level of conflict in the family rose higher, the tension in the marriage increased as well.

Bob and Laura were determined not to let this continue, how- ever. Unlike most couples, they had anticipated that their children might feel insecure and try to disrupt their relationship once they were married. Rather than let things get entirely out of hand, Bob and Laura redoubled their efforts to support and communicate with each other. They set aside regularly scheduled times to be alone together each week and faithfully held to them. They were commit- ted to not allowing the children to come between them and talked about this directly with the children at the family meeting they held every Sunday night.

Tensions ran high in the new family for several months, but grad- ually Bob and Laura's efforts paid off. They were able to maintain their relationship as a couple despite their children's attempts at disruption. As it gradually became clear that none of the children could come between Bob and Laura, family conflict began to sub- side. Bob and Laura were also effective in communicating to the children that they were not going to lose their relationship with their other natural parent because of the new marriage. Both spouses were able to support the children's relationship with their other natural parents, and they acknowledged the need for children to spend time alone with their biological parent on a regular basis. Things gradually improved throughout the first eighteen months of the marriage and, by the end of the second year, the Martins were enjoying a harmonious family life and beginning to plan a new baby.

Children may place a direct obstacle in the path of the new cou- ple's relationship by disapproving of the marriage and trying to come between the newlyweds. This opposition makes it harder but even more necessary for the marital pair to carve out a separate sphere for their own relationship and maintain their primary coalition with each other. Parents should not expect their children to share their happiness over the new relationship because, as discussed in chapter 3, children often want their original parents to reunite. From their point of view, when one of their parents remarries their original parents are prevented from reuniting. Parents should anticipate children's resentment, and they can give children the opportunity to express their disappointment, anger, and worry. Although parents should talk compassionately with children about these concerns, children's disapproval of the marriage is not a reason to cancel it.

Some single parents involve their children in selecting and approving their dates and may even solicit their children's approval of their marital partner in the belief that they help themselves and their children by sharing this part of their life. A few parents may even go so far as to base their decision on remarrying on the children's choice of the new spouse. When this occurs, parents have made children responsible for an adult decision, but we have already seen that it is not in the best interest of children to be able to exert so much control over adult relationships. The decision to remarry should be left to the adults and should not include the children.

Another problem in establishing the marital coalition is the issue of loyalty bonds. All step-families struggle with the same question: Who comes first, the children, the former spouse, or the new spouse? It is especially hard for single parents to rearrange existing loyalties with their children to include the new spouse. New spouses often feel that they are being left out of the parent–child unit. Legitimate responsibilities to children must be met, and it is important to maintain a cooperative parenting relationship with the former spouse; however, it is also critical for spouses to meet each other's needs. Each partner must feel that the other is available and supportive. This responsiveness is a difficult task in step-families, however, because there are so many competing demands and responsibilities. Spouses frequently complain that "the children always come first, there is never time for me." This feeling of being put off or always coming second is one of the most common marital problems in step-families. The couple must set limits on their obligations to others and regularly set aside time to be with each other. If not, parent–child relations will suffer along with the marital relationship.

Step-families Are Different

Step-families are not the same as nuclear families. Because the nuclear family is the only model for parental roles and family relations that most of us have, too many adults try to recreate this traditional family style in their remarriage. As we have seen, adults can often approximate this model if children are under eight years of age or so when the adults remarry. With older children, however, initial attempts to share the parental role with the new spouse create conflict—which is why most stepfamilies have more conflict than nuclear families. Thus, step-families with older children should not try to be like a nuclear family, but should determine which parenting roles and family relations will work best for them. For example, one sibling may accept some guidance and discipline from a stepparent while another sibling accepts none. One stepparent may want to take on parental responsibilities with children while another may not. Step-families blossom when they respond to their own preferences and make the family what each member wants it to be, rather than trying to force it into the traditional nuclear family model.

Step-families also have more ambiguity than nuclear families because they need to evolve more of their own roles and rules. The guidelines for what to do are not as clear. For example, even something as basic as what to call another family member must be decided. There is no convention for addressing stepparents to fall back on. Should children call Mother's new husband Jim, Dad, Mr. Jones, Stepdad, Father? In response to this ambiguity, children should be encouraged to find their own names for family members. They should not be told how to address others, but should find what is comfortable for them. Further ambiguity occurs as the stepparent's role in the blended family has to be repeatedly redefined. The blended family will change significantly, especially during the first two years. To succeed, parents must have the flexibility to tolerate these ambiguities.

There is one final characteristic of step-families that parents should be aware of. Membership in the family and sharing a collective identity with other family members are not the same in step-families as they are in nuclear families. To function successfully, every family member must share in a group identity, and each family develops its own rituals for demonstrating who belongs to the family and who does not. For example, families demonstrate their shared identity with each other by attending a Fourth of July picnic together each year, or by taking pictures on Christmas morning that may be kept in photo albums year after year. Some families set places for absent members at the Thanksgiving dinner table as a way of acknowledging everyone who belongs to the family. These are examples of the many different traditions families use to define themselves as a family group: "We are the Harris family."

Membership in the step-family is more open than in the nuclear family. For example, noncustodial parents may regularly participate in the step-family. They make decisions about the children and may take an active role in determining the direction of the children's lives. This situation, which brings an outside person—a third parent—into the step-family, does not occur in nuclear families. Also, children of divorce usually belong to two families. They often have strong ties to their other parent and feel a part of the other parent's family as well. The step-family is not their whole world.

There are also more comings and goings as children leave the step-family to visit or live with their other natural parent. If that parent has remarried, stepbrothers and stepsisters may also enter into the equation. As a result, the question of family membership is central for these children: "Who is in my family? Who belongs, and who doesn't?" Children feel agitated and insecure until they have answered that question to their satisfaction. These children have trouble feeling that they can belong to two families and maintain ties to both of their biological parents. Parents can help children resolve this conflict by repeatedly reassuring them that they can belong to both families at the same time and do not have to choose between them.

Guidelines for Parents

In summary, I would like to emphasize four guidelines for parents in step-families:

1. Children will see the stepparent as less of a competitor if adults can support the children's relationship with both of their natural parents. This appreciation of the importance of children's relationships with their natural parents and of the need for private time with them should be repeatedly expressed.

2. Partners in a remarriage should drop the expectation that stepchildren and stepparents should love each other. This expectation puts an unrealistic burden on both children and stepparents. Further, when older children are involved, stepparents should move into the parenting role very slowly, if at all. An older friend is a more workable role than parent in many cases.

3. It is important to remember that parents choose to remarry, whereas children simply become part of a step-family. Thus, parents must take full responsibility for the decision to remarry. Children should never be given the power to decide whether or not their mother or father remarries. While parents should talk with children about the marriage and reassure them about the concerns they may have, the responsibility for the decision to marry should be left to the parent and should not be shared with the children.

4. The remarried couple needs to establish their own primary marital relationship. This statement does not mean that the natural parent is supposed to love the spouse more than the children or place the needs of the spouse before the children. Nor does it suggest that the parents should never disagree in front of the children. It means that the couple needs to put other demands on hold, find time to be alone, and prevent children and others from repeatedly coming between them and disrupting their relationship or ability to communicate. Establishing a primary marital bond also means that each feels secure that the other is looking out for him or her and will be available and supportive if called upon. Many forces impinge on the new marital relationship, and these efforts must be made to maintain the marriage. There will be more cohesion in all step-family relationships when the new spouses can maintain their own relationship as a couple.

I wish to end this book by acknowledging once again how difficult divorce can be. Most of us have grown up believing that most change and conflict have been relegated to our youth. We often expect that once we marry we are grown up and that life will settle down and proceed at a steady pace. Divorce shatters this myth, however, along with our ready assurance of who we are and where we are headed. Thus, during the crisis of divorce, many parents truly feel that they don't know who they are, what they're doing, or where they're going.

It can help to realize that divorce is not the end of the line: It is the end of a marriage and the beginning of a new phase of life. However, divorce suddenly forces us to see ourselves in new ways. This disruption of our identity and life plan is even more difficult when, as adults, we are not only responsible for ourselves but for our children as well. Although it may take a year or two to fully regain your equilibrium, you can create a new and satisfying life for yourself and your children. During this period of adjustment you can also change and grow as an individual and as a parent. Divorce can offer you a chance to become more independent, flexible, and tolerant. As you learn that you are able to cope with life's problems, you may find that you are capable of becoming a better parent as well.

As you struggle to manage your life in a period of self-doubt and turmoil, your children are grappling with similar feelings and thoughts. They look to you for guidance, reassurance, and love. By explaining children's fears, concerns, and misconceptions, I have tried to help you understand some of the things your children cannot communicate very well on their own. You can use this understanding to help your children successfully adjust to divorce, and there's no time like the present to begin.

Index

About the Author

Edward Teyber, Ph.D. is a child-clinical psychologist. He is Professor of Psychology and Director of the Community Counseling Center at California State University, San Bernardino. He is the author of numerous research articles on the effects of marital and family relations on child adjustment as well as articles on parenting and post-divorce family relations for the popular press. His textbook for therapists is entitled *Interpersonal Process in Psychotherapy*. In private practice, Dr. Teyber specializes in post-divorce family relations. He lives in Los Angeles with his wife and two sons.